A Better Way

John Barrow

Printed & Manufactured in the United States of America
1 2 3 4 5 6 7 8 9 10

ACKNOWLEDGMENTS

I wish first to thank my wife Lindsey who told me over and over again throughout the years that I needed to write my own book. After trying six ghost writers, none of whom was able to sound like me, she finally convinced me to try it on my own. And so I did. She has always remained steadily by my side, firmly planted, through the good times and the bad. God richly rewarded me with a great helpmate and wonderful friend. Praise Him for all that He has done. I am blessed beyond measure.

Thanks also to the "A Better Way" Team—Lisa Neville, Brother Phillip Bowden, and Brother Jerry Powel—all of whom are my greatest allies and devoted servants of The Most High. The ministry would not be what it is without these three true servants of Jesus Christ. My Quams. ☺

My faithful assistants Sharon Barnett and Matt Geipel, who always pulled the wagon when I was down for the count and trying to recover. Their faithfulness has remained true throughout the years and is summed up in the verse that says "a friend who sticks closer than a brother." Where would I be without you two? I love you dearly.

The founder of Teen Challenge, David Wilkerson, who is at home with the Lord now, but surely not forgotten. Thank you, Brother David, for answering the call and going to help the "least likely." Where would so many people be right now had you not been obedient to the voice of the Lord? Oh, what an outstanding example you were of what God can do through a soul who makes himself available. Thank you for being that example.

Chaplain Ray. Your books and testimonials are more valuable than gold. Reading about the hope, the peace, the healing, and all the other great benefits that come to a man who surrenders and looks to Jesus Christ for his rescue, was like finding water in the middle of the desert. Thank you for writing the stories that so helped to change my life. Thank you for being more than a chaplain.

FOREWORD

AS A TROUBLED teenager in Fulton County juvenile, I picked up a book written by a man named Chaplain Ray. Ray Hoekstra was the Chaplain at San Quentin, one of America's roughest prisons, Ray was not only a chaplain, but a writer as well, and while being in the middle of so many notorious men he took advantage of his abilities and wrote a series of books that told about the lives of the men whom he had become so personally involved with. Each book would start by telling a little about the man's life before he went to prison, what kind of crime he committed to get there, what his experience was like while doing his sentence, how he met God in the midst of it all, and then finally what he did after he made parole. Reading these books helped inspire me as a young man to want to be like these men. They prompted me to want to be a better person and pointed me towards this same God whom they had found.

Looking back over the years that followed, I remember trying to find Chaplain Ray's books wherever I found myself doing time. These simple messages of redemption, which lit up like small lights along my dark path of wrong choices, played a big part in my decision to alter the course of my behavior. They became stepping stones that finally helped me get out of the pit I found myself in. They were used to help this unstable young man finally find his footing. And for that I have a great debt to repay, which is why I have been compelled to share my story as well—

so that it might help someone else, such as yourself, to see that there is light at the end of your tunnel and to inspire you to press on and take hold of a much better way to live. My hope is that this book will remind you that no matter where you may find yourself in life, your story can have a happy ending, too. No matter how dark the clouds may appear, you can rest assured that just above them there is a bright blue sky, even though it can be hard to see sometimes when your vision has become clouded.

My prayer is that this book will do for you what Chaplain Ray's books did for me and that the same heart that was in him will become yours also—the heart of our Lord and Savior, Jesus Christ.

Thanks, Chaplain Ray, for sharing the power of the testimony and for the stories you left as a reminder of God's redemptive power. Thanks for being a light in the middle of a dark cold prison cell and allowing that light to warm the hearts of many hardened men. That light still shines today and for that we will be eternally grateful.

CONTENTS

PAIN AND JOY

"Each heart knows its own pain.
And no one else can share its joy."
(Proverbs 14:10)

P AIN AND JOY. All human beings experience these two emotions—though not in equal measure. They are opposites in every sense, as far as the East is from the West. Webster describes pain as that which causes physical or emotional suffering and to experience great distress or torment. Joy, on the other hand, is to experience keen pleasure or delight caused by something exceptionally good or satisfying; to feel festive, happy. King Solomon, the man who penned Proverbs 14:10, was intimately familiar with both emotions. In the book of Ecclesiastes he confessed that "whatever my eyes desired I did not keep from them. I did not withhold my heart from any good pleasure" (Ecclesiastes 2:10). But, then in Proverbs he cautions: "Have you found honey? Eat only as much as you need, lest you be filled with it and vomit."

Most of us, like King Solomon, have found this to be true. Just a tad bit of joy or that "keen pleasure" that something "exceptionally good" brings can end up making us sick if we're not careful. *If a little is good then a lot will be great and more is always better,* we tell ourselves. It's kind of like the Lay's potato chip commercial that teases "bet you can't eat just one." It could be something as "seemingly" small as that extra potato chip that keeps piling the weight on, watching that TV show that screams conviction or being around someone you know is not healthy for you. Or, it could be something as big as having a few too many drinks, popping another pill, doing another line of coke, or seeking that next sexual encounter. Whatever our joy-and-pleasure-producing-thing is, we convince ourselves that all will be well if we can have just one more, just one more time—as an old rock 'n' roll song put it "just one more fix, Lord, might do the trick."

The next day, though, or the next week, maybe even the next year, we find that our one little "joyful occasion" has started a roller coaster ride of the most excruciating pain. What started out as just a little pushing of the envelope has turned into a major issue. That one more potato chip had a fishhook hidden in it that we just couldn't see or didn't want to see. But now it's too late. The hook is in too deep and we just can't spit it out, which causes us to feel the pain of taking the bait once again.

Sometimes making that wrong choice can keep us longer than we want to stay and cost us more than we want to pay. Most of us never actually intended to bite off more than we could chew. It just turned out that way. Most of us never set out to self-destruct and cause harm to ourselves and everyone around us. It just unfolded that way. Most of us thought we could handle a little joy ride only to find that our inability to "turn it off" like some do sent us careening out of control and landed us in a ditch full of pain.

One of the loneliest, most painful places a person can find himself is in a cold, dark prison cell. It is a place very few ever intended to go. Little boys dream of growing up to be policemen, firemen, cowboys—anything but convicts and inmates. But, because some of us could not stay within the boundaries, we found ourselves in too deep. What started out as an "I can handle it moment" ended up with another painful consequence. What started out as a happy moment ended up with another sad ending. And the question we keep asking ourselves over and over again is "why?"

- Why do we continue to do the very things that bring our old familiar friend "pain" back into our lives?
- Why do we find ourselves making the same old lap over and over again?
- What is it about us that causes us to pick door number 1 when we **know** it should be door number 2?
- Why can't we be like normal folks and just get and stay with the program?
- How do we turn into Satan's puppet again and again knowing that he will make us dance as he has so many times before?
- Will I ever get off of this vicious ride and stay off?
- Will I ever solidify my walk and stabilize?
- Will I ever get my feet beneath me once and for all?
- When will I quit hurting myself and causing all this collateral damage to those around me?

These are the questions many of us ask as we walk out our journey. Just as the Apostle Paul cried out in the book of Romans chapter 7, trying to make sense of it all, trying to figure out why we do the things we do. In this book, I want to share how God answered these questions for me and how He can surely answer them for you as well and give you a life more abundant and fulfilled than you have ever imagined. Whether we are in a physical prison, behind steel bars and two-foot-thick concrete walls, or in an emotional or mental prison, we cry out for relief. We cry out to God and ask Him please—*please*—to deliver us from our pain, to deliver us from that same of lifestyle. We say, "Help me learn from my mistakes. Help me be a better person. Take away these desires that rage within, Lord. Please deliver me from my life-controlling issues. Have mercy, O God, and deliver me from myself once and for all."

These were my thoughts over and over again. Every time I found myself in YDC, the county jail, the state penitentiary, and finally holed up in solitary confinement, I would ask these questions. It seemed that

I could never break free from the chains that had me bound. Every time I walked out of those prison doors a free man, I vowed that I would never return. I just knew that I would not make those same old bad, destructive choices again. But every time, I did. I would get out and hold steady for a while … but before long I would find myself lonely, bored, and discontent. Then I would call an old friend, go back to an old hang out, or simply drink a beer or two. And before I knew it I was back at the races doing the same old thing. Shortly thereafter, I would find myself once again in some jail cell crying out "why?"

It was during these times of brokenness and desperation, however, that God began to speak to me. It was during these times when all seemed lost that I eventually found what I was looking for. Over the course of spending some eight years of my life in and out of prison, punctuated with countless trips to solitary confinement, I finally fell to my knees and surrendered to the call that was so evident on my life. God had to do to me what He had done with Moses—allow him to experience the wilderness with all its harsh surroundings, stripping him of all his own abilities, disarming him completely, breaking him, and humbling him, only then to recalibrate, reshape, and remold him so that He could finally use him.

Thank God, the Potter, for the Potter's wheel, and for the loving hands that never fail to work the sticks and lumps out of these old pieces of clay. To God be all the glory, all the honor, and all the praise.

CHAPTER 1

A SHAKY FOUNDATION

I WAS A VERY rebellious youth. By the time my dad came home from Vietnam, when I was around 5 years old, I was already a handful. I was raised by a 16-year-old mother and her mother, my grandmother. Their intentions were good and they loved me dearly, but my being an ADHD child was simply too much for them. Back then they didn't have words like ADD or ADHD— they just called you "bad." And with no male role model in my life I got off to a really bad start. By the time my dad got home a good portion of the foundation had been built. Those first 5-6 years of life are very important in a child's development. I have been a contractor now for 20 years and know firsthand that if the foundation is not built correctly, I will most likely have problems with the entire structure. Starting off with the right conditions is very important in anything we do.

John Barrow
childhood photo

I have often wondered what would have happened if I had been born to and raised by a Christian mom and dad out on a farm somewhere in the middle of Idaho picking potatoes. Or in some Amish family going to church, fishing with my dad, milking cows, smelling the hay, watching the sun rise, and reading books instead of watching a television. *Would it have made a difference in the way I turned out? If the foundation had been built differently—solid and square—would I have been a better young man?* I realize that it doesn't make any difference at this point, but I have always asked myself and God that question. *Am I a product of my environment or was I destined to be where I am today?* And every time I go there in my mind I always come back with these two conclusions. The first is that I probably would have had a much better chance at success as a young man and most likely would have had a much less painful life. The second, however, is that if I had gone that way I would not be here today writing this book, trying to give you a positive word and letting you know that all is not lost if you fail. I would not have learned the life lessons that I have so that I can share them with you and others to help you on your way. I would not be able to remind someone like you that what God does for one He will do for two, and what He has done for me He will surely do for you. That is the wonderful thing about God. He always extracts the best from *any* given situation. So, at the end of the day it does not do much good to look back and ask why? But, only to look forward and be assured that nothing in our lives will ever be wasted as long as we keep our eyes fixed on Him and continue to look beyond our past and present circumstances.

Serving Two Masters: Sex and Drugs

Growing up I was like a lot of inquisitive teens excited at the prospect of trying anything—at least once. Unlike Bill Clinton, I *did* inhale. I inhaled a lot. As a matter of fact I inhaled gasoline fumes, glue, aerosols, marijuana, cocaine, heroin, LSD, alcohol, THC, and anything else I could get my hands on that could give me a feeling of euphoria. It is only by the grace of God that my mind can add 2 and 2 together today. I wasn't just a casual, recreational drug user. I was hooked before I even smoked my first joint. The truth is, I remember distinctly that I couldn't wait to get high. It was all I thought about other than sex. Drugs, alcohol, and sex were the top three things on my list. By the time I reached 13 I had experienced all of them and realized that I wanted as much as I could get.

My life was centered on how I could lay my hands on the next bottle of beer, the next mind-altering drug, and the next available female. Nothing else seemed to matter at all. Looking back I now realize how enslaved I was to my three masters. What bondage! I remember looking at the jocks in school who played sports and the other "normal" kids who weren't part of our clique and thinking they were so weird, so backwards. I now see who was weird and backwards: *me.* I was the one who missed the prom because I was in YDC. I was the one who could have been a good athlete but chose instead to stay intoxicated. It was I who chose instant gratification over methodically building a well-balanced life. Oh the things we learn as we grow up, and how clearly we can see when we turn our eyes on the past.

By the time I was 14 I had committed a host of crimes—burglaries, buying drugs, selling drugs, stealing cars, to name a few. Atlanta's Fulton County Juvenile became my home away from home and prison was beckoning in the distance. I was heading downhill fast with no desire whatsoever to even use the brakes ... until one night, while incarcerated, I was exposed to something and someone that began to slow me just a little. It was really the beginning of my end, though I didn't even know it at the time.

I will never forget the night. It was burned into my heart forever. A man named John Koth came to speak to a bunch of us rebellious teens at Fulton County. John had been a gang leader in New York City but was now a born-again Christian. He had just completed a program called Teen Challenge and was traveling around the country telling young men everywhere about the freedom he had found through Jesus Christ. He told us how many times God had spared his life and assured us that God wanted to spare us as well. He told us that God loved us and had a plan for our lives.

As I listened to John speak, something began to touch me. I remember just wanting to go back to my cell, shut the doors, and cry. Deep down in my soul I knew I wanted what he had, but I just couldn't grasp it. When he spoke of his freedom, he was so full of joy and passion. I remember thinking: *If I could just grab hold of that I will be all right.* If I can get what he has then my life and desires would change. At that moment I would have given anything—*anything*—to have the joy that he had and to be able to feel the way he felt.

If only I could have continued to feel that warm feeling I felt that night I know I would have changed forever. But feelings never last. All too often they fade away and we are consumed once again with the "old life." We forget the moment of our visitation and revert to our old familiar nature. Oh how important it is to look back, pause, and remember, to manually rewind those tapes when we heard God's voice and were moved to the point of change and to think back on how we felt when were exposed to the truth—the real truth—the one that began to set us free. It took me years to figure out that real peace and joy come from commitment and dedication, not simply from just one emotional response to an inspirational truth. The emotional response is just the spark that lights the flame. The flame must then be tended so that it will not be extinguished due to lack of care.

Change of Venue: Teen Challenge

The next morning I requested a meeting with my probation officer, Ken Corley, who just happened to be a Christian. In fact, Ken was the one who had orchestrated John Koth's visit. Some 38 years later Ken and I are still friends. When Ken arrived I asked him about John Koth and the place that he had come from, Teen Challenge. I wanted to know if that place might be an option for me instead of going to the Augusta Youth Detention Center on another burglary charge.

I knew that even if Ken approved it, the judge most likely would not. But somehow things worked out. My request was approved, and I soon found myself on a plane heading to Teen Challenge. Needless to say, I was very grateful for the change of venue.

Soon after arriving, however, I discovered that I was not prepared for what I found. I felt as though I had walked into a monastery and gone back in time 10 years. There was old furniture scattered about and one small black-and-white TV with an antenna wrapped in tin foil. The only programs we were allowed to watch were church and an occasional sporting event, that is, *if* you could get the thing to even pick up a signal.

No secular music was allowed at all unless you sang it to yourself. Try going from ZZ Top and Led Zeppelin to Dallas Holm and Bill Gaither. It was like doing 30 days in the electric chair every time they turned the radio on. No tobacco was allowed. Of course that wasn't hard either after being used to smoking a pack a day. There were no phone calls for a month. No reading materials other than the Bible and a book called *The Cross and the Switchblade.*

You got up at 5:00 a.m. and did devotions. Then you did your chores and went to Bible class. That night you did some more chores and more devotions, went to class, and then went to bed because lights were out at 10:00 p.m. The next day you got up and did it all over again. Somewhere in the midst of this hectic schedule you ate two to three meals (depending on what day of the week it was) and heaven help you if didn't like powdered milk, powdered Kool-Aid, and even some powdered food. There was very little free time and very little privacy. Sunday mornings and evenings were spent in church. Saturday was the only day of the week that provided "entertainment," an occasional softball game or a swim in the river.

Though I hadn't really known what to expect when I arrived, it surely wasn't *this.* As a young teenager I just wasn't feeling it. I had been used to driving 100 miles per hour and now I felt as though someone had put me in an Amish horse and buggy. At the time, however, I was so glad to be out of juvenile lock-up and the cold hard confines of a state-run institution that I more or less gladly adjusted to the new way of life.

Before long I forged some close relationships with a few of the other guys. The guy I admired most was Danny Martinez. Danny was a Puerto Rican from the streets of New York. He had been heavily involved in gangs. He was quite a bit older than I, and was probably in his early 30s.

Danny was one of those guys with a heart the size of Texas and everybody loved him. He did, however, have a rather short fuse for foolishness and nonsense. He was the "alpha male" of the home. He had been a golden gloves boxer for the state of New York and had numerous knife-wound scars on his body from a slew of gang fights with switchblades. He was definitely the real deal and a stand-up guy. Danny became a great friend to me and a guy whom I really respected and looked up to. He was

At Teen Challenge as a young man

extremely serious about his relationship with God and was giving it his all to truly change his life and become a better man.

One night after we all got in bed and were lying in our bunks in the dark, I was talking to a guy one bunk over from me. He had only been there a week or so and it was clear that he was trouble. He was around Danny's age and a rather large man. We had been kidding a little as we were talking back and forth and he said something that was kind of unbelievable. I can't even recall what it was, but I just said something light-hearted like, "Man, you're crazy...."

About 15 minutes later, just as I was falling asleep, I felt somebody approach my bed. It was the big guy. In a low harsh voice he said, "If you ever call me crazy again, I'll kill you." Well, needless to say that confirmed that he was. I don't remember getting too much sleep that night. I was a fairly tough kid for 14 years of age, but I knew my boundaries, and this guy was way outside of them. He was twice as old, twice as big, and definitely twice as crazy as I was. Anyway, the next morning I told Danny what happened, and all I know was that later that day when I was walking through the house I passed the big guy in the hall and I am here to tell you that he looked at me as though he had seen a ghost—a ghost that he never wanted to see again. Shortly thereafter, the big guy left the program, but before he did he never again looked at or said anything crazy to me again. Danny just told me that he had "talked with him." Danny actually went on to marry the founder of the ministry's daughter and became the husband, father, and man of God that he truly wanted to be. I will always think of him as a protector of people—the very thing that Jesus was. The very thing that I wanted to be as well.

Satan's Foil: The Cabin of Iniquity

Another vivid memory from Teen Challenge was the day in the river that bordered the back of the property. That old river was where they baptized the men and that we were allowed to fish in as long as we had an accountability partner. That river was used to help change my life forever.

It all started when two other guys—Juan and Keith—and I went down to the river to fish and swim one day. Juan and Keith had become my two best friends at the time and we were always together. Juan was a Hispanic kid from California who was in gangs and Keith was a local guy who was waiting to go to court on a pretty heavy charge. Both were older than I and had been there longer.

On this particular day we grew a little tired of fishing and swimming. We needed some more adventure. I suggested that we go further up the river, all the while knowing that we were not allowed to swim beyond the property borders. Moving upstream well past what was allowed, we spotted an old cabin sitting on a hill.

We paused wondering if anyone in the cabin was watching us. Being the youngest and maybe most foolish one, I got out of the water, made my way up the hill, and climbed up onto the cabin's porch. Peering through the windows I quickly discovered that it was not a place where someone lived on a regular basis but only on occasion when someone wanted to stay to do some hunting or fishing. So I began jiggling the windows and doors until I pried one open. Once inside I motioned for Juan and Keith to join me.

Upon further examination we discovered a treasure trove of forbidden fruit: cigarettes, beer, liquor, *Playboy* magazines, and more. Needless to say, since none of us had ever been able to say no in the past, we didn't break tradition and say no this time either. Without our spiritual legs firmly planted underneath us, the temptation was just too great.

Such behavior was my pattern and this soon led me to become desensitized. I began to lose interest in the classes, the Bible, and everything else. It's just like the word says, "You can't serve two masters. You will hate the one and love the other." My spiritual eyes, even though they had been partially opened, began to slowly close—although not completely. It was impossible to become totally numb to the presence of the Lord in that place. The same power that caused me to respond to John Koth's message in Fulton County was the same power that would not leave me completely alone there, either, even though I seemed to be slowly slipping away. (In Isaiah 55:11, God says: "My word ... that goes forth from My mouth ... shall not return to Me void, but it shall accomplish what I please, and it shall prosper in the thing for which I sent it.") Although my flesh still said *no,* my spirit unknowingly cried out *yes.* That's why the Apostle Paul said "for the good that I will to do, I do not do; but the evil I will not to do, that I practice" (Romans 7:19).

But why? Why do we continue to get side-tracked when we know where we need to be going? Why when exposed to truth do we continue to reach for a lie? What is it about that one tree—the tree of the knowledge of good and evil—that God said not to eat from that makes it so that we can't keep our hands off of it? What is so puzzling is that God gave Adam the *whole* Garden of Eden with a multitude of trees. Eden was a climate-controlled environment, with no need for air conditioning or central heating. Adam did not need to search for food because the garden was filled with unspoiled fruits and vegetables. He didn't have to buy clothes because the naked human body before the Fall was nothing to be ashamed of. Adam did not even need to search for a spouse because God made Eve especially for him. And if all that were not enough, God then gave both of them control over every living thing. The only request He made was that they not eat of the fruit of *one* tree—just one single tree.

Why? Why was all the rest not enough? How is it that we can so quickly lose our focus and our way? How can we walk out the doors of a prison, find freedom from a life-controlling issue or whatever had us bound, and *so quickly* forget all the gratitude that filled our heart and the way we felt at the moment of our deliverance? Why can't we seem to stay in that place of being grateful—grateful for the freedom, grateful for the small things, grateful for our deliverance? What is it about the human heart that prevents it from being happy for long? Why is it that the forbidden fruit always seems so succulent, so delicious that we are willing to sacrifice everything else—every other tree, every other comfort—to have it?

A Storm is Brewing

Well, after a few weeks of making numerous trips upstream to that cabin of iniquity, something happened that etched itself in my mind forever. One day an angry storm erupted. Ominous black clouds filled the sky. Serrated lightning bolts slashed the sky, thunder claps boomed all around as the rain fell in great sheets and strong winds swirled all around. It was one of those storms that you look up at and realize just how big God is and how small you are and that sends you heading to the cellar. Well, I want you to know that God surely proved to me that day just how big He is and how small I am. Somewhere in the middle of all that thunder and lightning a large bolt struck right square in the middle of that little cabin on the hill and burnt it slap to the ground. All that was left was charred wood, smoldering embers, and three young men who got the fear of God in them. We had been hiding our little excursions for some time, and every day and night as we joined with the others to pray, sing, and study we knew that we were living a lie and that God was not pleased.

I learned right quick that the Lord will not let anything come against His work and that He will always protect His church and His ministries. The Bible says that the fear of the Lord is the beginning of wisdom. It is neither a portion nor the fullness of wisdom. No. The fear of the Lord is the *beginning*. For us to be even a little wise we must understand that our God is an all-consuming fire who does not bear the sword for nothing. Fearing God is a good sign that we are beginning to understand the heart of our Father and giving Him the respect that He so rightly deserves.

After that storm hit and the cabin burnt down, I stayed in the program for another month or so before running off with another boy and wound up in Roanoke, Virginia. We managed to get a job and a place to stay but eventually got arrested and locked up for selling marijuana to an undercover detective. Soon thereafter, we were extradited back to Atlanta and put back in detention to await further charges.

CHAPTER 2

LIKE EVERY NIGHT IS FRIDAY NIGHT

A FTER SERVING MY time, I ended up at home again and continued on my downward spiral. One night soon thereafter I was at a friend's house where a bunch of us were all sitting around getting high and a buddy of mine, Bobby, who is now in prison for murder, started talking about his new job and telling us how his boss would take all the money home in a black bag at night. He said that every night at closing time he would see him and one of his assistants put all the day's cash in a black bag and load it into his car. I don't know why Bobby began telling us that, but it was all I needed to hear. I promptly told him that I was going to rob the men. Because we were all high he just smiled and shook his head not taking me seriously. The very next night, however, I grabbed a CO^2 BB pistol, put on a jacket with a furry hood, pulled a stocking over my face, and went and sat behind a dumpster at the rear of the restaurant waiting for closing, which was about 11:00 p.m.

At some point Bobby came out back to dump the trash and saw me behind the dumpster. I said "Hi, Bobby" and he looked at me as though I was an apparition and said, "You were serious?!" I said I sure was. I looked at him and could tell he was having a hard time swallowing and connecting all the dots. He quickly turned around and scurried back inside with a very startled look on his face. Around 10:45 I came out from behind the dumpster, went to the side of the building, and spied the front door until I saw two Chinese men walk out. Just as Bobby had said they were carrying a small black bag. I began approaching them slowly as they got into their car. The man in the passenger's seat was holding the bag so I walked to his side and, gripping the gun with both hands, ordered him to give me the bag. Playing like he didn't understand me, he put the bag between his legs on the floorboard. After a few more requests he was still acting as though he didn't understand English, so I let go of the gun with my left hand, aimed it at his head with my right, reached down and grabbed the bag from between his legs, yanked it out of the car, and backed away and took off running. To this day I am still amazed that I wasn't killed that night. For all I knew those two guys could have had a pistol under the seat or in the glove compartment and opened fire on me. Besides, I didn't even have any BBs in the gun.

I ran through the woods and found a pay phone and called one of my buddies, Rick, to come and get me. He was there in minutes and as we drove away we had to pass right back by the restaurant I had just robbed. As we passed by we saw police cars converging on the scene and it appeared that two of them had actually crashed into one another trying to get there. It was a world of flashing blue lights and cops running everywhere.

Somehow we drove right by and soon ended up at a Pizza Hut with a pitcher of beer, a large pizza, and bunch of cash. After counting the money I found that it was over $3,000. That was a fortune for a 15-year-old boy back in 1977. I thought I had died and gone to heaven.

Rick and I soon left the Pizza Hut, went home, gathered our belongings, and headed out to Ft. Lauderdale, Florida, somewhere around 2:00 or 3:00 in the morning. I am not exactly sure why everyone thinks the party is in Florida, but when a teenage boy thinks of getting wild it seems that Daytona Beach, Panama City, and Ft. Lauderdale come first to mind. Anyway, as we hit the expressway and headed south we weren't even out of the area good before we had blue lights behind us. Rick was driving and I was in the passenger seat kicked back with all the money in the glove compartment of his car. We pulled over pretty quickly when we saw the lights behind us because we felt pretty positive that it had nothing to do with the robbery

The patrol officer came to the driver's window and asked Rick for his driver's license and registration and then told us that we had a taillight out. No sooner had we breathed a sigh of relief than the cop asked me for my identification. So I pulled out my learner's license and handed it to him. He went back to his car and, after what seemed like an eternity, returned and told Richard "You are free to go." He looked at me and said, "You have a runaway warrant out on you." I told him that I was not a runaway and that there must be some kind of mistake. He didn't buy it. He handcuffed me and took me to Fulton County Juvenile, only to find out after calling my dad and checking the system that the runaway warrant was an old warrant that had never been purged from the system. So, they subsequently let me go a few hours later, but not until after Rick had left with all the money and with no way for me to contact him. Cell phones and beepers had not yet been invented. There I stood with only a few dollars in my pocket while my friend and my money were on their way to Ft. Lauderdale, Florida, to have a party of a lifetime.

You know, it always seemed to end up that way for me. I never got away with anything. It was like I was snake bit when it came to crime. Nothing ever seemed to turn out right when I did wrong. I was stopped at every turn and hemmed up in every corner. If the cops didn't bust me my parents would. All my friends would get away with murder, but not me. Their parents would come bail them out of juvenile. But not mine. Mine would actually take me there and drop me off. My friends could drink a beer, smoke a joint, and do whatever else they wanted and their parents would turn their heads and not look. My mom had every phone in the house tapped. She worked for BellSouth and had one of her friends wire the phones so she always knew what I was doing before I even did it. I look back from the distance of 30-plus years and thank God for a mother who cared enough to practice tough love with me.

She would often say, "Son, I'd rather see you locked up in jail than out here hurting yourself and everybody else around you."

Had it not been for her interventions I may not be here today. I thank God for a mother who loved me enough to always go the extra mile and one who obviously loved me more than I loved myself.

Seeing Beyond "The Now"

As a 50-year-old man with four children in my home, I can sometimes see in them the same ignorant and selfish patterns that I had. It can sometimes be scary as a parent. I am just now beginning to understand what my mother must have felt with me. I feel pain when my children suffer self-inflicted wounds that I cannot prevent. I feel distressed knowing they always have to learn things the hard way. I look at them and realize what limited vision they truly have. Their inability to see beyond the "now" can sometimes be very difficult. I remember being so caught up in my little world, with my little perspective, that I couldn't see the big picture. All I could see was what was right in front of me—my wants, my desires. *My my my, me me me, now now now.*

Though in all my own selfishness, I can honestly say that I never intended to hurt my parents. I never said to myself, "John, let's go get high so that Mom will cry," or "Let's go steal that car so that Dad will get upset." No, I did the things I did because in my mind that was what was going to "do it" for *me*—what would bring me the satisfaction I needed to quench my appetite and help me escape from a reality that I obviously didn't like.

My dad once told me: "John, you live like every moment is Friday night." I just couldn't seem to find peace anywhere unless there was music, some kind of substance to alter my mind, and a female companion. Those were the essentials without which I could find no contentment. It was almost as if those three things were out of the mix when God made me and unless I had them I felt handicapped. I found it so hard to be alone with just me—just me and no drugs or booze, no girls, and no music. That was one of the beauties of "solitary confinement" in prison. Once they shut that door behind you, you are faced with you and you alone. You are forced to sit there and think. After sleeping a few days you can't seem to sleep anymore, and that's when you just lie there and begin to process stuff. You begin reflecting on the past. You start to ask yourself questions. And it was during times like these that God began to speak to me and show me why I did the things I did. One of the biggest things He revealed to me was my inability to be content with the simple things in life. The things that I didn't even see were the very things that mattered most: God, creation, family, true friends, honor, loyalty, and much more. I had been going so fast that I had totally missed the most obvious.

A few years back my wife and I took in her handicapped brother, Mike, to live with us. We live on 50-acre plot in a very rural part of the county. Mike is nearly 40 years old, has never been married, never had a girlfriend, never driven a car, had lived with his mom and dad all his life, and worked at Pizza Hut for 20 years bussing dirty tables and cleaning up everyone's mess.

When he first moved in with us I would see Mike outside sometimes and as he would walk by the window, all by himself. I would think to myself how lonely he must be not having anyone to hang out with. I would see him swimming in our pool alone and think *he must be depressed.* I would think about him cleaning off tables at a Pizza Hut for 20 years and wonder how a person could do such a tedious and unpopular task and never quit. So one day a few months after he came to live with us I noticed him standing alone, and I walked up to him and said, "Mike, how are you doing?" Mike answered with a smile that never fades and his standard answer "Great!!! How are you doing, John?" So I said "Same here" and then asked him, "Are you OK? Do you enjoy living out here with us?" Mike smiled again and said, "I sure do. I love it out here. I'm content, John. I've learned to be content."

Well, talk about getting an education. At that moment I went back to school. I stood there looking at him and wondered how in the world he could be content. There I was married, kids, cars, Harleys, money, and a plethora of other stuff, and I wasn't sure I could even answer that question the way he did—*content*. How does a man who has so little find such contentment? How does a man who has never experienced some of the greatest things in life give an answer like that? Mike had obviously found something.

The Apostle Paul had as well. From a prison cell, far worse than the prison cells of our day, he said, "I have learned in whatever state I am, to be content." *I have learned to be content in all situations.* (Philippians 4:11). Contentment is the key to winning the race. What helps keep us anchored is being able to find joy in the mundane and simpler things in life and not having to have the stimulation that comes from what the world has to offer.

It's funny how a man who finds himself in prison becomes acclimated to that environment. When he first arrives he is usually distraught due to his new living conditions. But after a while he slowly begins to conform. He starts going to bed at a certain time, getting up at a certain time, looking forward to the nights when they serve lasagne instead of soy burgers. He begins to enjoy playing cards, going out on the yard instead of just sitting inside, exercising, reading a good novel, etc. He no longer requires all the extreme stimulation he needs on the street. He begins to enjoy the simpler things in life. The small things become enjoyable. He finds contentment in the middle of a place that has stripped him of what he once thought of as the essentials for living the good life. *Why is that? What is it about the perspective shift that happens once we are stripped or forced to do without? Why can't we just grab hold of it naturally?*

Contentment. Finding contentment is the key to open many of life's doors.

So Where's the Loot

Getting back to Rick who made off with the restaurant money. As I said earlier, in those days there was no way to find him other than to go and physically search. I had no idea where to look for him in Ft. Lauderdale and I had no way to get there, so all I could do was stick my thumb out, hitchhike down there, and give it my best shot to find him. I knew the odds were pretty good that he would be in some bar or at the beach, so I was confident I would succeed in finding him if I could just get there. But, again, before I could get out of town the next day, two Fulton County detectives paid my dad a visit at his office. They asked him my whereabouts and if I by chance I had a cast on my right arm. I did. I had gotten in a fight with a German guy at school and broken my right hand on the back of his head. That's one reason I was holding the gun so tightly with both hands, so as to hide the cast from the man I took the bag from, but when I reached down and yanked it out of the car I had exposed the end of the cast. The cast was a dead giveaway, and my dad assumed correctly that I was the guilty party. He led them to me before I could hit the road for Florida and once again they stopped me in my tracks.

I soon confessed and pled guilty to armed robbery and was sentenced to two years in Milledgeville YDC. I was very thankful that they didn't try me as an adult because I would have gotten a mandatory five-year sentence to be served at the state prison in Alto, Georgia. I will always be grateful that I managed to avoid doing time in Alto, which was a notoriously violent prison.

When I arrived in Milledgeville they assigned me to cottage 8, which they called "crazy 8" due on account of all the long-term guys assigned to it and some of its crazy students. I will never forget the day I arrived at intake. The way it works is that you get herded around for the next 48 hours or so by another student who himself has been locked up for a while. (He's usually a rather large guy with an ominous appearance; big and mean-looking is the only requirement for the position. When you get into population, however, you find out that nobody likes him because he's a snitch and not really tough at all. Then you really feel like a dummy because you let him order you around for two days.) You are then ordered into what looks like a shower for washing cattle and told to get naked. They then turn a big bug sprayer designed to kill crabs and lice, which 99.9% of the inmates don't have, on all the hairy parts of your body. The way it kills them is by burning them to death right along with your privates and your armpits. You stand there on fire until the spray hose-wielding "tough guy" decides that everything on you is dead. This makes you really want to kick his butt the next time you see him on campus because when you do you know he's looking at you and thinking, "I made you dance a jig butt naked and you sure looked stupid while you did it." No wonder the position had such a high turnover rate. It's hard to keep a tough guy looking tough when he has a black eye all the time.

Anyway, I began to settle in and soon became acclimated to the new environment. Cottage 8 was actually one of the best cottages in the place. I guess since they expected us to be the worst they just overlooked a lot of the petty stuff that the other cottages got busted for. Cottage 8 was known for its athletic ability and its tough guys. I actually played on the basketball team that won the state championship just before I was released. Sure, I sat on the bench more than I played, but I was there. It was hard to hang with all the guys from East Lake Meadows, Perry Homes, and some of the other inner-city places where they were born with a basketball in their crib. I was just glad to be on the team. If I remember correctly there were only two of us white guys who could even hang.

The guy who was supposed to be the "top dog" in the cottage was a black kid from Savannah named Stanley Hall. Stanley was a great athlete, as well as a pretty good fighter, even though he was missing his two front teeth. Some guy who had left just before I got there had punched him in the mouth, knocking his teeth out and sending him down a flight of stairs. Stanley must have taken it pretty well because it didn't seem to have even put a dent in his pride. He just had the state of Georgia make him some false teeth that he would take out every time things got ramped up. I guess he just figured since he could get free teeth he would talk as much smack as he wanted. Stanley and I got along pretty well and never ended up in a fight. I guess you can say we had a mutual respect for one another.

A Pancake Breakfast to Remember

I never started a fight with anybody, but I never walked away from one, either. Not because I didn't want to but because you couldn't. I remember getting into three or four fights in the two years I was there. This was not bad considering we were all a bunch of hard-headed young men. The fight I remember most vividly was with a kid named Kenny Lark. One morning on the way to breakfast Kenny accidentally stepped on the back of my heels as we were walking in the mandatory single-file line to the chow hall. Well, I turned around expecting him to say "I'm sorry" or something of that nature, but instead I got a "What you gonna do about it?" look. So I just let it go knowing that fighting would cost me 14 days in solitary confinement. Once we got to the chow hall, however, he did something else that extinguished that thought. After getting our breakfast from the serving line we were required to take our food to the table, take it off of the serving tray, carry the serving tray to another designated area, and then come back to the table and eat. Well it was while I was gone to put my tray up that it happened. Mr. Kenny thought he would do something to my pancakes. When I returned I found I was sitting right across the table from him and right next to the guard who was on shift at that time. This just so happened to be a Sunday morning, and we always looked forward to Sundays because we got pancakes for breakfast, so I sat down and I immediately started to eat. As I looked up from my plate with a mouthful of pancakes, however, I noticed that a few of my buddies were looking at me kind of strange. They didn't say anything but were giving me these weird looks and then looking down at my pancakes and then back at Kenny. I knew something was up but I didn't know what because we were not allowed to talk in the chow hall or we would get written up. Besides, Kenny was sitting there looking at them so they couldn't communicate freely anyway.

We finished our meal and went out and as we were lining up to go back to the cottage two of the guys who were looking at me strange at breakfast told me that Kenny had spit in my pancakes as I went to put my serving tray up. I looked hard at them to see if they were kidding and I could tell that they weren't. This was one of those points in prison when you have to put all your options on the scale and begin to weigh them. You think things such as: (1) If I hit him I am most likely going to solitary for 14 days and possibly extending my stay at this 5-star resort, (2) if I don't straighten it the other guys are going to think I'm weak and I may end up eating spit every morning for breakfast, and (3) if I do opt to retaliate what are the chances that I can take the guy so I can avoid not only eating his spit but possibly getting my butt whipped as well? So after processing all of the above you usually reach your conclusion, which most often means that you must try to hurt the guy as fast as you can and as bad as you can. Unfortunately, that is usually the best path to take even though it is not the most civilized. You cannot live around a bunch of men who don't respect you. Plus, you also have to live with yourself. Respect is a major priority in the prison system.

So, after processing it all, I decided that I was willing to do the time in solitary, get extra time added to my stay, and possibly get my butt whipped in order to level the playing field and have a little get-back with Mr. Kenny. It really was a vicious cycle and the very reason that so many men who start out with small sentences end up doing much longer ones for retaliating against guys like Kenny. He should have apologized for stepping on my heals and just enjoyed his pancakes and the Sunday afternoon watching football and playing spades and so on. But no, he had a bent place in his mind and probably felt that life was just not what he wanted it to be. Maybe he had been dealt a bad hand as a child and still couldn't figure out how to play the cards. Maybe he was just mad at the world and didn't know how to deal with it. Maybe he just wanted to prove something to himself. I don't know. I'm not sure what it was, but as a young man doing time I learned that it was best to stay away from guys who thought like that. Ones who simply didn't care whether they got out or not. The Bible warns us to stay far away from an angry person. Angry people are adept at hurting not only themselves but everyone around them. And, prison is full of angry people who are mad at God, mad at their parents, mad at the world, and mad at everybody. The more they hurt on the inside the more they want to hurt others on the outside. It is tragic to see people who are bound to a ball-and-chain that they can't seem to get free of.

Speaking of angry, though, I was unfortunately angry as well. The more I pondered the fact that I had just eaten a man's spit while he watched me do it—no doubt smiling inside all the while as I savored the syrup mixed with his nasty saliva—the more I wanted to inflict bodily harm on him no matter what the possible repercussions would be. So as we were walking in cadence and everyone was on the same foot—left-right, left-right—I took a good right foot step and then came around with a solid right hook knowing that my momentum and Kenny's momentum going together would add a substantial amount of impact to his nose or his mouth or whatever part of him I could connect with. It worked. Kenny's little legs began to buckle underneath him when I connected with the left side of his head, and as he tried backing up under a flurry of punches he fell to the ground. The formation of men began to break apart over the unexpected disturbance and the guards began running toward us. Before long the "fight" was broken up and we were separated until we got back to the cottage. And as unlikely as it was, I was not placed in the hole due to the fact that I had two witnesses come forward and testify that they saw him spit in my pancakes. That was one of the very few times that I escaped solitary for fighting or some other infraction. Solitary confinement was actually a common occurrence for me in those days and continued throughout most of the eight years in total that I spent behind bars.

The thing that landed me in the hole most often in YDC was that I liked to leave without permission. I recall how when I first got there I would look around at the guys in the room wondering who was fixing to try to escape. I honestly thought that every man in there would be posturing for a getaway. I recall looking across the dorm and thinking "why would these guys not want to escape from this place? How can they just sit here and not constantly be thinking about breaking out? After getting to know all of them, however, I found that only one would be interested in breaking out. His name was Billy Summers. Billy was from the Warner Robins area and was in for a pretty serious crime. If I am not mistaken he had shot his dad and almost killed him.

Billy was angry as well. He wore a shoe that was built up about two inches due to the fact that when he a child his dad had beat him with a 2' x 4' and had done permanent damage to his back. I guess Billy felt like he didn't have much to lose and knew that he wouldn't be getting out anytime soon. As with most escapes, we studied the timing of everything and how the guards were wired, we plotted how we would steal a car, steal some money, go to Florida, get some booze, get some drugs, and find a few girls who wanted to party. We were two kids living in a fantasy world, of course, but oh how real it was to us at that time. Our vision was so skewed due to the fact that we had never really learned or experienced living in the real world with a "normal" view of reality. That was as foreign to us as aliens from another planet. Looking back at 50 years old I realize now just how different I was from the status quo. Everybody I thought was abnormal was really normal and I was the one on another planet.

So Billy and I waited for the right time and broke loose one day from the field house, a place where we were allowed to shoot basketball and play pool. We ran and jumped the fence and made our way through the woods and farms surrounding the place. We were not gone long before we were caught. I think we made it a whole 48 hours. If I recall correctly we made it to the following night before we were surrounded by flashlights and bloodhounds in a field. I remember Billy and me huddling together because we were freezing due to the cold and we were lying under a blanket of vines and kudzu as we watched the flashlights and heard the dogs barking all around us. I distinctly remember a guy talking into a radio: "They're in here somewheres; old Blue smells 'em." I want you to know that old Blue was so close at one point that had I wanted to I could have reached out and grabbed his ear, but they did not find us that night. To this day I don't know how we made it out of that field but we did. Billy and I were shaking so violently from the cold and the fright that I knew that dumb dog could have heard our teeth chattering even if he couldn't smell us.

As it turned out, though, the next day a farmer with a shotgun captured us. Word around camp had it that if a farmer caught you they got a sack of flour and some beans. I'm not so sure whether that was true or not but that was the story. Also those people around the YDC were serious about capturing escapees because a few had escaped one time and had murdered an older couple in the area. All I remember is that I was glad to be back in custody. Between not having any food or water, being torn up by barbwire and thorns, being frozen half to death, and being horrified by old Blue and Bubba, I felt as though I had been rescued when I was thrown in solitary. As most of us often do, however, within a short time I forgot about the pain and got back to "normal." I finally got out of the hole a month or so later and adjusted for a while.

It wasn't long though before I was ready to try again. I talked with old Billy and he said that he had had enough and wasn't feeling it anymore, but I found another guy who was game and we went the same way Billy and I had gone before, back through the woods and farms. It had not been as easy trying to get away this time. After my earlier escape they had reinforced the razor wire and added an alarm system with a huge siren in the middle of the campus. Every guard now had something resembling a garage door opener on his side, and if anyone escaped the guard was supposed to push it to sound the alarm that alerted all the security to come running. It made it a lot harder to get away although we managed to do it. But, just like before we were caught within a few days and again I was glad to be back. I was exhausted and half dead from lack of food, water, and sleep. Back to the hole for another 30 days and then back to population. This time I stayed for about a year until I just couldn't stand it anymore. The desire to be free was killing me. It wasn't that the conditions inside were bad, it was that my mind was outside that fence, and every day that went by I felt more and more like a caged animal. Like a lot of 17-year-old males with testosterone levels of a Brahman bull I felt like I had to escape.

Unlike my two previous attempts, I decided to head directly towards the town of Milledgeville instead of through all the farm land. When we left the cottage for dinner and the guard was locking the door, I bolted. I knew that since my last escape they had added a tighter mesh wire to the top six feet of the fence to prevent escapees from getting their fingers through the holes, so I stole a stack of forks from the kitchen and jabbed them into the wire so that I could pull myself up. I then threw my jacket over the razor wire so as to limit the inevitable slash wounds and climbed over. I don't think security was prepared for me to head directly towards town because I'm pretty sure no one had ever tried that before. I just figured that since I had struck out twice heading the other way I had nothing to lose. I somehow made it there and wound up behind an old hotel.

I bummed a dime from someone and called my grandmother and aunt, who were two of my biggest enablers. I told them what I had done and asked them if they would come and pick me up. After a bunch of murmuring they finally agreed. I asked them to bring a wig, some make-up, a bra, etc., so I could disguise myself. I waited under a bush in the dark for about two hours before they finally showed up. I hopped in the back seat and scrambled to put on my disguise and then we finally pulled out into the road. Cops were everywhere, just as they had been the night I robbed the Chinese restaurant. I just sat up in the back seat and looked at them as we drove out of town. I couldn't believe my grandmother and aunt had actually done it. They say the fruit don't fall far from the tree.

Hurricane Frederick had just hit Mobile, Alabama, about this time, so I headed down there to mix in with all the out-of-state construction crews. My old buddy Rick, the one who took all the Chinese robbery loot and went to Ft. Lauderdale, joined me in Mobile and we started working for a roofing company. We actually started making pretty good money, got an apartment, and I bought an old car. I managed to stay out of trouble for a minute or two even though we were doing our usual drinking and drugging.

Until one morning when we were on our way to work in my car I had just bought, we approached a school crossing with a police officer directing traffic. Well, I had three problems on this particular morning. One, I was late for work. Two, I had just stopped at McDonald's and got an Egg McMuffin and a cup of coffee, which was wedged between my legs. Three, my master brake cylinder had a slow leak in it so I had no brakes. I was manually using the emergency brake to stop the car until I got to work and then planned on filling it up with more brake fluid. Well, the cop waved us on through at first, but then all of the sudden he threw his hand up for us to stop. So as I reached down to grab the emergency break lever, hot coffee was spilling all over my privates (remember that McDonald's was later sued over the temperature of their coffee). At the same time I was watching the cop right by my window as I passed slowly by him staring at him with this bizarre look on my face. It was a look that said, "Oh no, I just screwed up." It is awfully hard to have a convincing look when you are all bent over in a fetal position holding yourself and your mouth is wide open trying to suck in oxygen due to pain that is racking your lower extremities. I can only imagine what my face looked like as I slowly rolled past him by about 10 feet.

The cop walked over and I rolled down the window. He said, "Son, do you have any brakes?" I replied, "Sure I do." He then told me to press down on them. I pressed the brake pedal but, trying to be clever, I was careful to avoid pressing all the way to the bottom. The cop asked me to step out of the car. He got in and found out for himself that I was lying. So he took my license back to his car. The whole time I was praying that nothing would come back on the check. A few minutes later he returned and said, "When's the last time you seen Milledgeville?" Well I knew that I was busted and had no chance of getting away in a car with no brakes. So they locked me up and let Rick go with my car. So, for a second time, I went to jail and Rick walked away with his hands full. He seemed to get paid for just hanging around me, like I was the gift that kept on giving. I wonder who took care of him when I was in jail. The truth was, he had been a good friend for a long time. One time my dad got tired of me sneaking out at night and going to my girlfriend's house so he put bolts in my windows from the outside so that I couldn't get out. Rick would come down around midnight, however, and let me out and then come back around 4:00 a.m. and bolt me back up. I guess I owed him.

I ended up being extradited back to Georgia on a plane and sent back to Milledgeville. And this time they were done fooling with me. They put me in solitary until I finished my sentence about three months later. It was a miracle in itself that they didn't add any more time to my sentence. I was one of the most troublesome teens they had come through there. All the guards had nicknamed me "Rabbit" and watched me like a hawk everywhere I went.

Looking back I see a mixed-up kid who had no concept at all about life and was running from God. I was looking for fun in all the wrong places. As I write about this troubled youth, some 35 years later, it's as though I don't even know what made him tick. Those feelings of rebellion and lewd behavior seem so foreign. It's as though I was another person—a lost person.

As David prayed in the Bible, "Lord, forgive the sins and errors of my youth" (Psalm 25:7).

O God, thank You for not holding my sins against me and for allowing me to live through it. Thank You for covering me during those rebellious years and not allowing the enemy to take my life. Thank You for the cross and Your Son Jesus Christ who bore my sins and became the remedy once and for all.

Thank You for sparing this man's life.

CHAPTER 3

A FEW YEARS ON THE OUTSIDE

O NCE I WAS released from YDC and got back home I had every intention of staying out of trouble, but that was short-lived. I ended up in a drunken brawl in the middle of Peachtree Street in downtown Atlanta and got locked up for public intoxication and disorderly conduct. It just so happened that I was fighting with, of all people, my friend Rick. I guess I could psychoanalyze myself and my behavior and say that subconsciously I was mad at him for taking my stuff every time I got locked up. But that wasn't it. It was just one of those stupid things that happen sometimes when you drink and act crazy. Once again, I went to jail and Rick went home. *And guess what?* I think he drove my car.

A Stint in the Army

As soon as I sobered up I called my dad and begged him to come bail me out on the promise that I would join the Army. He did. (That was the only time I ever remember him doing so. Maybe he felt sorry for me because I had just served two years.) So after doing a minimal amount of research on what the Army had to offer I signed up to be an Airborne Ranger and was sent to Fort Benning, Georgia, for infantry school. It was a perfect fit. I did great in basic training, completed advanced infantry training, went through jump school to get my wings, and finally made it into the Ranger Battalion. I never realized just how much stress a human body could endure without collapsing. And as if the rigors of military training were not enough, I decided to party every night on top of it. I soon found myself straddling the fence and gradually started slipping deeper and deeper. Once I got more freedom I began heading right back into old behavior. A few beers in the evening led to late nights out, doing drugs, and then back into addiction, which caused me to start the same old pattern of getting in trouble with the governing authorities again. Although I knew where I was heading I just couldn't seem to stop.

My first small infraction came one day when I was in Mount Rainier State Park. A couple of park rangers pulled me and a few other guys over and gave me a ticket for some infraction that I can't recall. I think it had something to do with my van or not having a sticker that signified I had paid to enter the park. I really can't remember, but as soon as I pulled away from them I threw the ticket they had just written me out the window. Somehow the park rangers saw me do it, jumped in their truck, and raced to pick up the pieces of the ticket. They then caught up with us before I could get out of the park and wrote me another ticket for littering. Something tells me that I might have made history with that one—getting a ticket for littering with a ticket.

A short time later, while I was doing some amphibious training in Coronado Beach, California, where the Navy Seals train, I got in another fight with some Marines in an on post club. I ended up with an Article 15 citation and was placed in the stockade for about a month. After I was released I went and asked my Commanding Officer if he would allow me to leave the Army early since we were not in war time and he said yes. It was rather easy to get out of the military back then because the enlistment time was only two years and I had been in more than half of it. I had seen others do it and it worked for me as well. I was awarded an honorable discharge—how, I don't know. I have never been proud of that decision, and it has always grieved me that I chose a party over a military career. To be honest I should have never left the military. I was born for it. I could have achieved great things had it not been for my messed-up priorities and shallow thinking. Just doing one year in the Infantry, Airborne, and Ranger training has been one of the most valuable things that I have ever done. Even though I didn't retire out of it, I did walk away with a tenacity that I didn't even know was possible to attain. I have drawn on it over and over during my bouts with prison, trials, and sickness. It has served me well over the years and I would highly recommend it to anybody.

Looking for a Safety Net: Starting a Family and Business

After leaving the Army I ended up staying in the Fort Lewis area for a while and wound up marrying my first wife, Laurie. Our marriage lasted for about a year. We moved to Georgia shortly after we married and lived with my parents for a while. My plan was to stay there until I could get on my feet and rent a house. Before that could happen, however, Laurie caught me seeing another woman, Debbie, who would eventually turn out to be my second wife. Laurie left me a few days after the shocking discovery and flew back to Tacoma, Washington, pregnant with my son Joshua. Again, it was all about me.

I married Debbie some months later and things were decent for a few years. We had a little girl named Hollie and started going to church some, and I basically leveled out for a while. I started making decent money selling cars and running a small trucking company. Then one fateful day a guy I met while selling cars gave me some cocaine, and that was the beginning of the end. Along with my occasional drinking and notoriously weak constitution, I soon wound up back at the races. Debbie had left me numerous times over my substance abuse, and I had always been able to win her back, but she just couldn't take it anymore. We divorced and she later married a pastor who eventually left her for another woman. In the wake of this betrayal, Debbie fell into major depression and started using anti-depressants and pain pills. She passed away in her 40s from a prescription drug overdose.

My daughter Hollie has been through the ringer as well. She was in and out of jail on drug charges and various other poor choices. Praise

God, at the time I am writing this book she has stabilized somewhat and is now married with a child. During her prodigal years, my wife and I adopted Hollie's first three children and are now raising them in a Christian home. We send them to a Christian school and have them involved in our church. I am doing the very things with Hollie's children that I should have been doing with Hollie. I was just so sick myself that there was no way I could have helped her. I had thought when Debbie married a pastor that Hollie was in good hands, but thanks to his immoral choices she probably lost all faith in God as a young girl. One dad was in prison and the other was preaching Jesus while cheating on her mother. So my daughter Hollie was just another child dealt a bad hand as the sins of the fathers were passed down from generation to generation.

Oh, how it all connects together.

Romans 5:19 says, "Because one person disobeyed God, many became sinners. But because one other person obeyed God, many will be made righteous." The Apostle Paul was speaking of Adam and Jesus and how Adam's wrong choices cost you and me and so many more. It is a great example of how our wrong choices trickle downhill and affect so many.

But, it also encourages us by reminding us that Jesus made a right choice and because of that we can find grace for *our* wrong choices just as Adam did. The beautiful part about it now is that it will not take another flood to wash the earth of all its sin or another burnt offering to get God to forgive us. Jesus Christ has paved the way once and for all, and we can now find forgiveness at the foot of the cross just like the sinner who hung right beside Him.

A word to the multitudes of men and women with children who are in similar situations today. You have made some wrong choices and their effects have been far-reaching. You lie awake on your bed wishing that you could do it all over again, wishing that you had just one more chance to "get it right." Now I don't know if you will be granted that privilege or not, but I do know this for certain: *If you will call on the name of Jesus and turn from your old life of sin, God will begin to heal you.* His promises are true and His desire is to heal your broken heart and repair what has been broken. But understand that being healed may not always be exactly what you think it is. It doesn't mean that you will not have some regrets or that you will forget the past completely. It does mean, though, that as you begin to truly reach out to Him you will find a place of peace in the middle of it all. God will help you process it better so that it does not consume you, and He will enable you to find value in your trail of tears. I know that is hard to understand how value could come out of such sorrow, but God always works like that if we will come to Him humbly, change our ways, and begin to live for Him. He is the master at making lemonade out of lemons. Just watch Him work. The Bible assures us that God will mend our broken hearts and that joy will come in the morning. The first step towards freedom is to ask Him for forgiveness and then forgive ourselves, just as so many others have before us.

One of the best examples of forgiveness in the Bible is King David. I encourage you to read and study David's story (recorded in the Bible books 1 and 2 Samuel, 1 Kings, and 1 Chronicles). David was a man who slew the Philistine giant Goliath with a sling and a stone, led Israel for many years, wrote the book of Psalms, was in the bloodline of Jesus Christ Himself, and was, according to the Lord Himself, "a man after God's own heart." Yet, as he was known as this great man of God, David committed premeditated murder and adultery.

We must ask ourselves two questions here. The first is: *How God could forgive David for such a travesty after He had entrusted him with so much?* David had to pay a great price for the sin he committed. Every action brings a reaction. The reaping-and-sowing law is always in effect. Most who are reading this book right now are very familiar with the consequences of wrong choices. You make a wrong choice, you pay a price. That's the way it is. But the thing about it is that the Lord never repays us as our sins deserve. His discipline is always smothered in love. He doesn't discipline the way we do. He never does it in anger or resentment. The second question we must ask is: *How could David forgive himself?* How did he live the remainder of his life carrying such a heavy burden—

knowing that he had murdered an innocent man for his only wife while he himself had a multitude of wives? What went through his mind every time he looked at Bathsheba knowing that her husband was buried right outside their home? How did he process such thoughts?

You see, we have all made our share of mistakes, and most of which are nowhere near as big as King David's. The Bible is full of stories of trial-and-error which prompts us to ask: *Why did God allow us to see the mistakes of our forefathers?* He did it for two reasons. The first is so that it would bring comfort to us when we fail knowing that others—even the "greats" of the faith—had failed as well. This gives us hope when we feel hopeless. The second is so that maybe, just maybe, we can see the results of the wrong choices in their lives and perhaps not make the same mistakes in our own lives, thus sparing us and others the pain.

One of the great sayings of Alcoholics Anonymous (A.A.) is that we must *get sick and tired of being sick and tired.* Oh how true that is. Although we can't drive forward while keeping our eyes fixed on the rear view mirror without having a wreck, we must make sure we glance back every now and then to remind ourselves of the past mistakes so that we won't make them again. That is all that God asks of any of us. Oh praise Him! Thank God that His mercies are new every morning and that He does not hold our sins against us. This surely brings hope to the hopeless and comfort to our souls. Oh what a friend we have in Jesus. He is here to set the captive free and bring beauty to the ashes. Your sins can be washed away, and the Bible assures us that God "will remember them no more." Isn't that wonderful news today? Isn't it comforting to know that this jury will *never find you guilty again?* In spite of the errors of the past—no matter how devastating they might have been—the verdict for the rest of your life will be "innocent." *How wonderful is that?*

At this point some may be saying, "John, all that sounds well and good and God may forgive me, but I just can't seem to forgive myself." Listen, if David could forgive himself and then God turned around and gave him the very woman (Bathsheba) whom he had murdered for, as well as place their son Solomon on the throne, then you should be able to forgive yourself. The key is to embrace the forgiveness and then to be done with the sin, forsake the sin, and then move forward with your eyes on the cross of Jesus Christ and the blood that has covered you and all your transgressions.

Sometimes it may also require you to go back and apologize to the people you may have hurt and to seek their forgiveness. But there it must stop. You are free. John 8:36 says, "For whom the Son sets free is free indeed." Romans 8:1 says, "There is now no condemnation for those who are in Christ Jesus." You are set free with no condemnation. Sounds too good to be true, doesn't it? That's why we need to celebrate our freedom by sharing the good news of Jesus Christ and letting others know that what He's done for one, He'll do for two, and what He's done for me, He'll do for you.

So forgive yourself, forgive others, and go do something positive for God and His people today.

Going Off the Deep End

After my disastrous attempt at another successful marriage, I kind of went off the deep end. I quit selling cars and lost my little trucking company. I ended up working as a bouncer in a couple of the bars on Old National Highway and was doing the "tough guy" thing. I had been studying martial arts and actually fought in what was known at the time as the Omni, a 20,000 seat arena in Atlanta. I was still trying to prove something to myself, still trying to measure up, and still trying to get applause from some invisible audience. I took home a different woman just about every night in hopes of filling the void. I was seeking approval and fulfillment because I had no stable identity and low self-esteem. I ended up in such bad shape that I lost everything I owned except the clothes on my back. I fell so low that I actually slept in a cardboard box as well as a dumpster in Daytona Beach, Florida. And after countless trips to various county jails, county prisons, drying out at Georgia Regional Hospital and the VA Hospital, sleeping anywhere I could find,

I landed in jail on an armed robbery charge for holding up another convenience store.

By this time other charges were pending in various counties as well. I had already served numerous small sentences for DUI, violation of the

Georgia Controlled Substances Act, burglary, disorderly conduct, simple assault, and other charges. Not to mention the plethora of crimes I committed for which I didn't get caught. So when I landed in the Fulton County Jail on this sentence, I pretty much thought I had hit the bottom. It is amazing how low some of us can go before we surrender. I was like a runaway freight train heading for hell and I was the conductor. When I look back and see all the pain I was going through in those years, I realize that I was probably one of the most miserable men on earth.

The "Prodigal" Days

I was running from myself and trying so desperately to get away. I was also running from something else and I knew what it was, the hounds of heaven. They had been hot on my trail for almost 10 years. I had tried everything under the sun to shake them but I couldn't. Ever since I had listened to John Koth and went to Teen Challenge they had been pursuing me. They were relentless and oh how glad I am that they were.

Prison Was One of the Best Things that Ever Happened to Me

I know that may sound crazy to some, but prison was one of the best things that ever happened to me. An old saying in prison that men say to each other is: "Man, they rescued you." Meaning that when they locked you up they delivered you from your own worst enemy—*yourself.*

I have a ministry now and will talk more about it later, but one thing I try to get the parents of incarcerated men and women to understand is that if they continue to enable their sons and daughters (especially those with substance abuse problems) by giving them money or a place to sleep it off or bonding them out of jail, more often than not they will find that they have just added nails to their coffin. Be reminded of the Parable of the Prodigal Son. This is not John Barrow's analogy but Jesus Christ's. In Luke 15:11 Jesus said:

"There was a man who had two sons. And the younger of them said to his father, 'Father, give me the share of property that is coming to me.' And he divided his property between them. Not many days later, the younger son gathered all he had and took a journey into a far country, and there he squandered his property in reckless living. And when he had spent everything, a severe famine arose in that country, and he began to be in need. So he went and hired himself out to one of the citizens of that country, who sent him into his fields to feed pigs. And he was longing to be fed with the pods that the pigs ate, and no one gave him anything. But when he came to himself, he said, 'How many of my father's hired servants have more than enough bread, but I perish here with hunger! I will arise and go to my father, and I will say to him, "Father, I have sinned against heaven and before you.""

You see, when he had spent everything he had, was penniless, was so in need that he ate raw corn cobs just to stay alive, and *no one gave him anything*, Jesus says that "He came to himself." Don't you want your loved ones to "come to themselves"? Then take your hands off of them and let God do what He does best. I know that to stop enabling a loved one is easier said than done, but we must do it if we want to save their life.

We need to be more concerned with protecting them from themselves than we are about being popular with them. A lot of parents are either too busy to care or are more concerned with being liked than they are with doing what is best for their son or daughter.

Growing up, I had five really close friends—Cody Mills, Dwight Meyers, Richard Hunt, Eric Simpson, and Rick Smith—all of whom were dead by the age of 35 due to drugs or alcohol, except for lucky old Rick. The one tragic thing that all of my dead friends had in common was that their parents were enablers. They would turn their heads and pretend they didn't see, bond them out of jail, or pay lawyers to defend them even when they knew they were guilty. Had they left them in jail to feel a little of the pain that was a logical consequence of their wrong choices, to reflect on their mistakes, and to possibly grab a Bible to read out of desperation, they would most likely be alive today.

Listen to what the Bible says about discipline in Hebrews 12:1-11 (NLT):

"Therefore, since we are surrounded by such a huge crowd of witnesses to the life of faith, let us strip off every weight that slows us down, especially the sin that so easily trips us up. And let us run with endurance the race God has set before us. We do this by keeping our eyes on Jesus, the champion who initiates and perfects our faith. Because of the joy awaiting him, he endured the cross, disregarding its shame. Now he is seated in the place of honor beside God's throne. Think of all the hostility he endured from sinful people; then you won't become weary and give up. After all, you have not yet given your lives in your struggle against sin. Have you forgotten the encouraging words God spoke to you as his children? He said, 'My child, don't make light of the LORD's discipline, and don't give up when he corrects you. For the LORD disciplines those he loves, and he punishes each one he accepts as his child.' As you endure this divine discipline, remember that God is treating you as his own children. Who ever heard of a child who is never disciplined by its father? If God doesn't discipline you as he does all of his children, it means that you are illegitimate and are not really his children at all. Since we respected our earthly fathers who disciplined us, shouldn't we submit even more to the discipline of the Father of our spirits, and live forever? For our earthly fathers disciplined us for a few years, doing the best they knew how. But God's discipline is always good for us, so that we might share in his holiness. No discipline is enjoyable while it is happening—it's painful! But afterward there will be a peaceful harvest of right living for those who are trained in this way."

You see if Mom, Dad, Grandmom, Granddad, husband or wife, or any other loved one continues to harbor, help, and enable us, then they will only hinder the work that God is trying to do in our lives. Had my mom and dad not practiced tough love with me and allowed God to be God in my life, then most likely I would be buried beside all my friends. And had my grandmother and aunt not been such a weak link in my chain I probably would have gotten it together much quicker. I realize that most of these people who enable us truly love us, and some of them have hearts the size of Texas, but they simply don't understand what this is doing to us. If they don't understand then it is up to us to help them by toughing it out and not asking or expecting them to be our answer every time we need help. To survive and recover we must quit being so co-dependent on others and start being dependent on God—solely on God. When we intentionally look to God and not someone else as our source then we will begin seeing great things happen in our life. Oh what a friend we have in Jesus. He is perfect in every way.

CHAPTER 4

THE WAR IS ON

ORTUNATELY FOR ME, the grand jury would not indict me on an armed robbery charge based on the fact that they could not find a gun so they charged me with robbery by intimidation. Armed robbery would have landed me a minimum five-year sentence, but on the lesser charge I served only two and a half years. After sitting in Fulton County Jail for a few months I was sent to Jackson State Penitentiary—home to many notorious convicts as well as "Old Sparky," Georgia's electric chair. I had already been there once or twice on less-serious crimes so I knew what to expect. They strip you, wash you, shave you, spray you, and give you a bunch of tests to see how smart you are. The better you score, the more likely you are to get paroled sooner because they figure that you may be smart enough to keep your butt out of trouble if you choose to.

Someone had prepared me for one of the spelling words on the test before I took it the first time. The word was **pusillanimous**, which means "lacking courage or cowardly." Now while I'm no Harvard graduate I am definitely not the dullest knife in the drawer, either. But tell me, how many convicts in the Georgia prison system do you think would know how to spell *pusillanimous* and be able to define it. Now, remember, we in Georgia are right next to Alabama and that just isn't the kind of word we use down here. Can you here us inmates saying something like: "Big

Red, y'all's gang is nothing but a pusillanimous bunch of girls." No it would be more like "Big Red, y'all a bunch of !*^$##$^&(*(*&^%$@@ and we fixin to kick yo *&%%$#@!#^&*(!^. I guess the state of Georgia decided that if you could spell *pusillanimous* then you might be worthy of a quicker release. At least that was our thinking. I envisioned the Department of Corrections tagging your folder with a gold star so that when they began to consider your release date they would all look around the big table and nod at each other knowing that they were fixing to discuss one of the "gifted ones" who knew how to spell *pusillanimous*. Needless to say, I always made sure I knew how to spell *pusillanimous* even though I have never to this day used the word in a sentence (before writing this book) and had to open the dictionary in order to spell it just now. Another wonderful learning experience from the state of Georgia.

My final destination on this particular excursion was Buford State Penitentiary to serve out the final two years of my sentence. Buford was a very rough penitentiary in its day. It was actually a rock quarry where men would split rocks with sledge hammers all day. By the time I got there it was much more civilized, but it was still home to some of Georgia's most notorious criminals. My first bunk mate at Buford was a man who had murdered an elderly couple with a shotgun and robbed their little country store. I remember looking at him and thinking "what on God's green earth possessed you to do such a thing?" Of course I know now what possessed him—demons—the same things that influence us to do some of the stupid things we do. I admit, however, that killing people for no reason was and still is beyond my comprehension.

A Cell-Block Entrepreneur

As a prisoner I started off in the middle of everything. As far back as YDC I was playing tunk (a card game) for my dinner tray, my dessert, my nightly snack, and whatever else I could scrape up. Gambling stimulated my restless mind. By the time I got to Buford as an adult I was smoking and selling marijuana, making "buck," which is homemade wine using sugar, yeast, and potatoes, running parley boards and pools for football games, running a convenience store out of my foot locker selling items such as cigarettes, coffee, etc. Here's how the pricing structure worked: I give you two and when you get your money you give me three back, or sometimes four, depending on who you were.

I also ran nightly poker games. Poker games in prison are different from poker games on the streets. The winner was often the one who could cheat the best. I remember keeping a few cards in the back of my weight belt. I used to work out a lot and would always tell the other players that I needed to wear my weight belt for lumbar support while making my footlocker my nightly seat. Looking back on it I don't think anyone ever caught me doing it, either. I would surely remember if they had because a fight would have surely ensued. I was only in two or three fights during my two-and-a-half-year stay. If you can average only one fight a year in prison you are doing great.

Survival of the Toughest and the Smartest

Prison is a very unusual environment to say the least. It is a dog-eat-dog mentality and survival is typically based on two things: how tough you and how smart you are. Inmates all fall into one of three categories. One: **Those who are weak and stupid.** They end up on the sidelines like water boys who only come in when they are called. Two: **Those who are strong and stupid.** They buffalo their way through with force and intimidation usually ending up hurt or in the hole. Three: **Those who are strong and smart.** These are the ones who run the prison. They are usually the quiet ones, who are not often in the limelight, and call the shots from the rear. They tend to be a little older and wiser to the ways of the prison world because they have *been there and done that.*

What makes prison the roughest is all the young bucks who are trying to prove something. My guess is that 90% of prison violence comes from men who are 25 or younger. It reminds me of the joke about the old bull and the young bull on the hillside. They are standing there looking down on a pasture full of cows and the young bull looks over to the older bull and says, "Let's *run* down there and get us one of those cows." And to that the older bull replies, "Why? Let's just **walk** down there and get 'em all."

The young guys in prison don't think too much before they act. They just act. If it weren't for the older, more seasoned inmates who strive to bring peace to the place virtually any prison would be a complete mad house all the time.

One of the older guys that became a good friend of mine back then was a guy named Big Marshall. Marshall was a lot like me in my early days. He was always looking for a way to beat the system and outsmart "the man." Marshall was and still is a great guy, but like most of us he was his own worst enemy. He was serving a double life sentence plus 30 years. Though he didn't kill anybody his crime was heinous. He went into a biker bar, The Silver Ribbon, on Stewart Avenue in Atlanta, got drunk, hooked up with a girl, and ended up taking her into the woods and raping her. Based on his past record and repeat offender status they threw the book at him. Marshall was one of those guys who just couldn't drink. Alcohol and Big Marshall simply did not mix. When he was sober he would give you the shirt off his back. When he was drunk he would try to rip the shirt off of yours.

When I talk to men in my ministry now, I often use Marshall as an example of what *not* to do. About a year or two after I was released from prison, Marshall finally made parole after serving more than 20 years. I was doing pretty well by this time and bought him a truck, some clothes, gave him some money, and introduced him to a woman whom he married. The good times were short-lived, however. Within just a few months Marshall was back in prison for getting drunk and making terroristic threats. The same old M.O.—get drunk and break the law. He was then sent back to prison for a few more years. He got paroled once more, stayed out a few months, and went right back for once again getting drunk and acting belligerent. He is now still in prison and it looks like the Department of Corrections is going to try parole with him one more time in the near future. As I said, Marshall is a very lovable man but he simply cannot drink alcohol and stay out of prison.

Returning to the Vomit

It seems so crazy how people will return to the same thing that has caused them so much pain. The Bible says, "As a dog returns to its vomit, so a fool repeats his foolishness" (Proverbs 26:11, NLT). Why do we go back to the very thing that hurt us so badly? What makes us do things that we know have caused us so much pain in the past? How could a man serve 30 years behind bars for a bottle of booze? Some time back one of the prime time news shows aired a report about a mouse and cocaine. They put cocaine in the mouse's water bottle, and as expected once he drank a little he kept going back for more until it was all gone. They then removed the water bottle from his cage for a few days to let the cocaine get out of his system, and when they put it back in the mouse would not go near it. Sometimes even a mouse has more sense than we do. King Solomon, the wisest man short of Jesus who ever lived, said this in the book of Proverbs (5:11-14):

> "At the end of your life you will groan
> when your flesh and body are spent.
> You will say, 'How I hated discipline!
> How my heart spurned correction!
> I would not obey my teachers
> or listen to my instructors.
> I have come to the brink of utter ruin
> in the midst of the whole assembly.'"

Solomon is saying to us: *Stop!* Quit feeding your sinful nature. Stop doing those things that are bringing harm to yourself lest at the end of your life you cry and weep wishing that you had made better choices. Here is a letter Marshall wrote to me a while back that I share with the men I minister to on different occasions.

Hey John,

I pray this finds you and your family doing well. Thanks for the stuff you sent me. I really do appreciate everything you do for me. I would write to you more but I know how you must feel about me telling you about all my troubles.

John, I feel like it's about over for me. I'll be 65 in August, and I'm having all kinds of health issues going on with me now. I asked you once about coming to get me if something happens to me and you said you would. I am going to tell my counselor that it's OK if you do. I do not want to be buried on piss ant hill. [That is a place where they bury inmates when they have no one.] When I went to have the surgery done last month they ran some more tests and told me that they found more cancer. They told me that they could remove it if I wanted them to but my body is just now getting over what they did to me last time.

John, I just don't know. I've been trying to call you but can never get you. John, I'm really in trouble here. I have no one. I know, you told me. And I also know I done a lot of this to myself. I hurt no one but Marshall. But, John, I really need your help. Please send me a little money. I would like to have some things when they take me back to the hospital to have this cancer cut out. I hate to keep asking you for stuff, but you are the only one left that will do anything for me. Please keep praying for me. I pray every day now and I believe I'm all right with the Lord. I do my best not to do anything that's wrong. Do you think I'll be all right, John? It's a bad feeling. I ask for mercy and forgiveness all the time. I've never felt this abandoned and afraid in all my life. I sure would like to talk to you before they take me back to the hospital. I'll keep trying every day. If the calls stop then you will know that they took me back to the hospital.

Please have everyone pray for me. If it's not too much to ask, have someone send me a note letting me know how you're doing. I think about you a lot. I know you're doing good whatever you're into. Again, I hate to keep asking you for help, but you're the only one that will help me. Sorry is all I can say. I love you like a brother, John. I think about when I was there with you. It really hurts knowing how things got so messed up the way they did. It's hard to see when things are happening to you, but when you look back you can see it oh so good. It makes you want to kick yourself. I kick myself every day, John.

Thank you for being my friend.
Love you,
Marshall
Later I pray.

Do the Next Right Thing

I kick myself every day. I kick myself every day. Listen, we don't have to live a life of kicking ourselves! We don't have to live wishing that we had made better choices. If you are reading this right now you can begin to make those choices immediately. I tell my men in the ministry, "Men, just do the next right thing." It really is that simple. Make a conscious effort to do the next right thing. You see: **When the pain of holding onto something is greater than the fear of letting go, we will change.** That pain will push us towards surrender if we will allow it. For some, that first step is to drop down on their knees and let go. And then ask the God of the Universe, the One who made you from the dust of the ground, to come into your heart and save you from yourself and this world's vices. For others who consider themselves saved they may need to get as serious with God as they were with the devil. If you can give the devil—the one who wants to steal, kill, and destroy you—your all, then why can't you give Jesus Christ—the One who wants to give you life and give it to you more abundantly—your all?

Fighting the Good Fight

I am well aware of the struggle with sin. I put my pants on the same way you do and fight the same devil you fight. As a matter of fact every man in the Bible fought the same fight that you and I fight. Here is what the Apostle Paul says in his letter to the Romans (7:14-25, NLT) regarding the struggle with sin:

"So the trouble is not with the law, for it is spiritual and good. The trouble is with me, for I am all too human, a slave to sin. I don't really understand myself, for I want to do what is right, but I don't do it. Instead, I do what I hate. But if I know that what I am doing is wrong, this shows that I agree that the law is good. So I am not the one doing wrong; it is sin living in me that does it.

"And I know that nothing good lives in me, that is, in my sinful nature. I want to do what is right, but I can't. I want to do what is good, but I don't. I don't want to do what is wrong, but I do it anyway. But if I do what I don't want to do, I am not really the one doing wrong; it is sin living in me that does it.

"I have discovered this principle of life—that when I want to do what is right, I inevitably do what is wrong. I love God's law with all my heart. But there is another power within me that is at war with my mind. This power makes me a slave to the sin that is still within me. Oh, what a miserable person I am! Who will free me from this life that is dominated by sin and death? Thank God! The answer is in Jesus Christ our Lord. So you see how it is: In my mind I really want to obey God's law, but because of my sinful nature I am a slave to sin."

You see, most of us, like Paul, understand the war that we are in, but we don't all understand that the only way we will win this war is to allow Jesus Christ to lead the way. He can win the war that we cannot win! Once Paul acknowledged that he was in the fight of his life and realized that the Son of God Himself was on his side, listen to some of his other statements:

1 Corinthians 9:27: "I beat my body and make it my slave...."

2 Corinthians 10:5: "I bring every thought captive to the obedience of Jesus Christ...."

Philippians 4:13: "I can do all things through Christ who gives me strength...."

Paul openly acknowledges his weaknesses and failures but also tells us that we must continue to fight the good fight of faith. We must not give up and give in. We can overcome *if we so choose* when we have the Lord as our helper. It all boils down to this: *Am I willing to beat my body? Am I determined to bring every thought captive today? If I fall short, will I go back at it or instead throw my towel back in the ring as I have done so many times before?* We must get determined to press in and press on and not respond as we have when we failed in the past, when we said, "Well, I've screwed up so I might as well go ahead and keep screwing up." No! Instead we must resolve to look in the mirror and say, "You know that doing those things is wrong and that is not who you are or who you want to be, so stop it and let's try again."

King David said that God's "mercies are new every morning." What a wonderful thing it is to know that every morning you have a fresh new start when you get on your knees and start the day by asking the Lord to help and forgive you. We must remember, however, not to take that grace in vain and simply continue to play the get out jail free card every time we fall short. We can't just keep on sinning with the flippant attitude that tomorrow morning His mercies will continue to cover us. Hebrews 10:26 cautions us that if we continue to sin willfully when we know better then there is no sacrifice left for our sin, and 1 John 3:6 says that *"no one who lives in him keeps on sinning."* The Bible also tells us that the more we know the more is expected from us (Luke 12:48). As we grow and mature as Christians we should become more and more like our Father in heaven, and that involves an act of the will. We must do our part to practice the self-control that has been made available to every believer knowing and trusting that greater is He who is in me than he who is in this world (1 John 4:4).

In 1 Corinthians 10:13 the Apostle Paul said: "No temptation has overtaken you except such as is common to man; but God *is* faithful, who will not allow you to be tempted beyond what you are able, but with the temptation will also make the way of escape, that you may be able to bear it." Paul is saying to me and you and to men like Marshall and everyone else that in God we can find our strength to hold steady. He reminds us that what we face is no different from what others face and the truth is that *if they can do it, we can do it.* I don't know about you, but it bothers me when I can't measure up to the next man. When I see others say no to sin and temptation while I cave in to it, I feel like less of a man. But, when I pass the test and withstand the temptation I feel good about myself and hold my head just a little bit higher knowing that I won that fight and that Jesus Himself is looking to the Father saying, "Did you see that, Daddy? John just made another A on that test. He is doing it, Daddy. He is really doing it this time. I told you that he was going to whip this thing once and for all." Don't we all want an "atta boy" sometimes? Well, who better than the God of the universe to give us one? We can do it with *His* help.

I am praying and believing that the next time Marshall is paroled he will make it. I would like nothing more than to see him finish strong and grab hold of the prize that eagerly awaits us.

CHAPTER 5

SALVATION IN SOLITARY

About 12 months or so into my sentence at Buford, as I was getting acclimated to my new environment, something momentous happened that turned out to be one of the milestones of my life. I got caught selling some marijuana to another inmate and I ended up in my old home away from home, solitary confinement, for 28 days. They could no longer do the old "30 days in the hole" routine because the state had ruled it was cruel and unusual punishment. I guess they felt two fewer days would make it "all better" for us.

In the hole (solitary) I was given one meal a day—if you could call it that. The meal came with a slab of "God knows what" and two slices of stale Wonder bread (it was a Wonder that you could chew it without breaking a tooth). The slab of mystery meat looked like a piece of Spam on steroids. None of us could ever really figure out what they put in the stuff and that's probably for the best. Let's put it this way: If it fell on the floor it would just bounce back at you. I remember when a piece of the bread fell off the tray and onto the floor one day as we were being served. The serving cart wheel rolled over it, and immediately blankets were thrown out "fishing" for that lone piece of run over bread. One slice of white loaf bread was a very hot commodity because we were constantly hungry.

Solitary is a weird place. It can play tricks on your mind if you let it. I have seen men just start screaming for no reason, saying and singing bizarre, off-the-wall things, even wiping their feces on themselves. Solitary is the last punitive resort man has to offer short of the electric chair or lethal injection. It houses three kinds of people: (1) those who are mentally handicapped, (2) those who prefer to be in solitary rather than in the main population because of fear, and (3) those who cannot abide by the rules. I tended to fall under the latter category. As a matter of fact I refused to play by the rules and I continued to feel the consequences of my choices.

On this stay in solitary, however, something in me snapped. Abraham Lincoln once said, "I have been driven many times to my knees by the overwhelming conviction that I had nowhere else to go." Well, let me tell you that there is nowhere else to go when you find yourself in a prison inside of a prison. Solitary confinement is definitely at the bottom. That's why they call it "the hole." You've fallen as far as you can fall. Though sometimes landing at the bottom of a hole can be a good thing. It's like I tell the guys I work with now—the best part about hitting bottom is that you can finally get your footing. You finally have something to push off of and start climbing out.

I don't recall how, but this time I ended up with a Bible in my cell. I was 25 years old at the time and had not looked at a Bible much since I left Teen Challenge as a boy. Sure, there were occasions when I went to church with Laurie and Debbie when I was married. But there is a big difference between "doing church" and really digging into the word of God. When you're in the hole with nothing else to preoccupy your mind you can truly begin to digest what you are reading. So for 28 solid days I read that Bible from cover to cover and for 28 days I cried and cried. I don't know how to explain exactly what took place at that time, but I do know that for the first time in my life I truly surrendered my will and got serious about my relationship with God. My heart was truly pierced by the scripture and the Word finally became alive to me in the midst of all the pain.

Wanting to Change Teams

As I began reading about such men as Moses, Abraham, Isaac, Jacob, King David, King Solomon, Peter, John the Baptist, John the beloved disciple, the Apostle Paul, and many, many others, I saw myself slowly wanting to switch teams. The men I was reading about were *real men—* not some fairy tale characters or weak men. They were strong, trustworthy, reliable, honest, brave, and so much more. These patriarchs of old were the kind of men that I subconsciously saw myself as being. Governor Jesse Ventura, ex-Navy Seal and professional wrestler, once said, "Religion is a sham and a crutch for weak-minded people." Well, you know what I say to that? "Praise God, the truth is that I finally saw my need for a crutch because if I hadn't I would not have found a Savior and been rescued from my infirmity. Yes siree, I needed a crutch because I surely couldn't walk on my own. The Apostle Paul once said, "When I am weak then I am strong." *True strength comes only once you finally recognize your weaknesses.*

To put it another way, Clint Eastwood's character Dirty Harry said in his famous one-liner: "A man's got to know his limitations." Now I don't know old Clint's spiritual beliefs, but one thing I do know is that Dirty Harry was right. In my stay in the hole, I finally met my limitations. I no longer wanted to get my strength from what this world had to offer. I no longer wanted to kick against the goads; I no longer wanted to turn a stiff neck against reproof. I knew once and for all that I had turned the corner and finally embraced "A Better Way."

Right there in the middle of that cell I began to ask God to please help me be what I knew that He wanted me to be. I knew that this was a real conversion and not just another weak-willed attempt at living a better life. I knew that it would be hard to walk out on a life I had lived a certain way for the past 25 years, but I was so inspired by these great men and women of old that I had just spent a solid month reading about that there was nothing I wasn't willing to do or endure in order to be like them. And being the strong-willed guy that I was, I was convinced once and for all that I could now do all things through Him who would most surely give me the strength.

I was not dumb enough, however, to believe that such a dramatic change would not come with challenges. I knew that I would be tested soon after I was released from solitary and back in general population—and I was.

Changing Course: Giving Up the Rackets

Upon my release from solitary I was faced with several challenges all at once. The first was that I had been faithfully reading the Word in the hole with no distractions, which was simply not possible in a noisy dorm. So I began to get up with the kitchen help around 4:45 a.m. when everyone else was still asleep. I found this time of morning to be best for me, and I still practice it to this day. I tell the men I minister to that if they forget everything else I say to please never forget this one thing: *Get up early and get alone with your Father.* He wants to speak to you before the hustle and bustle of the day begins, and He wants to fill your tank with the fuel that you will need to make it through the day ahead. And, believe me, you will need every last drop of it before day's end.

Another thing that happened was that I found that I had to change the way I did things. I quit running poker games, parleys, making buck, smoking pot, and even smoking cigarettes. While I don't believe cigarettes or tobacco will keep you out of heaven, it's kind of hard to tell another person about the delivering power of Jesus Christ while you are blowing smoke in his face or pausing to spit out your dip. At least that's what the Lord told me. You can take it from there. I also had to change some playmates. The Bible says that bad company corrupts good character. And, knowing that my character was just beginning to change for the good, I knew that bad company might surely corrupt it before it had a chance to take root and grow. This was a bit of a challenge because I had a lot of friends. But when I put it in the scales and weighed it out, I soon realized that old "friends" had helped cost me my freedom many times before. There's an old saying that "birds of a feather flock together."

Well the kind of birds I was looking for after I got out of solitary was "free-birds" not "jailbirds."

I was looking for men who wanted to be not only physically free but spiritually free as well. It's not that I was too good for them or too Godly for them, but I just had to give myself some time to get my spiritual legs underneath me before I could help anybody else. That's the very reason why they tell you that if you are on a plane with a child and an emergency breaks out that you, the adult, put on your oxygen mask first—so that you can then help the child. You must get yourself stabilized before you can help anyone else. There will come a day when you will be strong enough to help others, but it will not be immediate. In the interim let God be your best friend and let Him send you new earthly friends who walk and talk like you now do.

I had not been out of solitary long when word came that a convict named Mike Jolly had arrived at our prison. Mike's reputation had always preceded him because he was a no-nonsense kind of guy. When these types of men arrived from other prisons they were typically kept in a holding cell for a week or so to let word travel through the prison in order to see if they had any major enemies or if anybody felt threatened by their arrival. Mike was a man who rarely started anything, but he did a very good job of finishing things. Mike, like Marshall, was from Cabbage Town and had grown up around Stewart Avenue in south Atlanta. He was about 40 years old and had spent a lot of his life in the notorious Reidsville State Prison. I had previously done time with his younger brother Ricky in Fulton County Jail. It turned out that Ricky was killed on a Harley while Mike and I were in Buford. I had never met Mike but had heard a lot about him. All I knew was that by all accounts he was considered to be "hell on wheels," so to speak.

After a while they released Mike into the general population and he took up residence in a bunk right next to mine. I will never forget that first night. I had become accustomed to hitting my knees beside my bed and praying before I turned in, something that I had started doing in the hole and had continued despite the risk of any public ridicule. I had already turned in when I remembered that I hadn't prayed, so as I rolled over and began to hop down I thought about Mike lying two feet away and wondered what he was going to think about me praying. I thought to myself "he's probably going to think I'm weak or something." I quickly brushed that aside, however, because the fact was that what God thought about me was now more important to me than what any man thought about me. So I got up and knelt down by my bed, prayed, and then hopped back into bed. As I lay there readying for sleep, I saw movement out of my left eye, and when I glanced over I saw Mike get up, drop to his knees, and start praying as well. Unbeknownst to me Mike had just recently gotten saved at the last prison he was in.

From that day forward Mike and I became good friends and remained so for more than 20 years. I actually got him a job and helped him get a truck when he finally got out some years later. Mike continued serving the Lord faithfully until last year when he passed away of leukemia. I helped officiate his funeral and oh what an honor it was to help bury a man who "got it right" and "finished well." I didn't have to scramble around trying to scrounge up kind words as I spoke about Mike's life the way I have done at the funerals of others who left this world on a bad note. In fact, I had a multitude of good things to say about him. Mike Jolly spent the first part of his life causing damage, but he spent the second part making repairs.

You see, it is not how you start but how you finish that counts. Thank God for the locker room in our lives and the chance to go in, sit down, and reassess the first half. The coach (Jesus) shows us the instant replays and we see just how we've messed it up and continually fouled people and fumbled the ball. We even notice that the bleachers are mostly empty because our fans have left the game in despair thinking there was no possibility of us winning. Most have lost hope in us on account of our many losses. But, oh how good it is to see a team come out in the 3rd and 4th quarter and come back against insurmountable odds to win the game. Well, that was Mike Jolly, and that can be you as well! Mike spent the last

25 or so years of his life being the kind of man that we all aspire to be—a devoted father, a loving husband, a man of God. I love you, Mike Jolly.

No Halo and Happily Ever After

Well, I wish I could report that all went well and everybody lived happily ever after from that night I met Mike until I was paroled ... but I cannot. I still had another year and a half ahead of me, and Mike had another four or five ahead of him. Life still happened, and we still had time to do in an environment where it was sometimes difficult to be Christ-like. It wasn't long until both of us were tested in a situation where there was no easy way out. One night our fellow inmate Little Red went to the shower and left his tobacco on his bunk. When he got out his tobacco was gone, and somebody told him that they had seen one of the new guys grab it.

The new guy happened to be black and Little Red was white. (We called him Red because his hair was red.) So Red came over to Mike, me, and two other guys and told us what had happened and asked us if we would "get his back" if he "straightened it." That was prison lingo for "I want to hurt this guy, but if anybody jumps in to help him will you guys help me?" So of course we committed to cover him, thinking that most people with a brain would know that the boy who stole his tobacco had it coming to him and would not defend wrong.

Well, let's just say that not everybody in prison seems to have a brain. Some stand up for each other just because they are in the same gang, or have the same skin color, or because they are homeboys (that is, from the same city), or just because they feel like it. You never know what to expect in such a hostile and dysfunctional environment. Well, I thought that Red, who had been on the boxing team in Reidsville, was just going to go over and start pounding on the guy, but I guess he didn't like the fact that this guy had stolen from him while he wasn't looking so he figured he would do the same to him. So Red went and got an industrial floor mop and broke the handle in half and went up behind the guy while he was sitting in a group of others watching TV and did a Babe Ruth number on the back of his head. It was as though someone had busted a grapefruit-size pimple with blood in it. I mean blood went everywhere and all over everybody who was sitting near the boy.

Somehow the boy managed to turn around, stand up, and start swinging towards Red. They told us later that he suffered a major concussion and mentally was never right again. Well the guards stormed the dormitory and took those two out, and we were all left in there with the tension so thick you could cut it with a knife. I don't recall exactly what transpired next, but somehow it turned into a black-white racial thing. I remember looking at a good friend of mine who was black and thinking to myself, "I am not gonna take a color side here. This is not about race but about right and wrong. And I don't think my friend will, either. If something goes down I pray that we can take a neutral corner and not get sucked in."

That was not to be the case, however. All I remember is that somebody screamed something about "them white devils" and then all hell broke loose. Several black guys began grabbing socks and loading them up with bars of soap to use like a swinging hammer. Another black guy grabbed a large pot of boiling water that was kept in the dorm for coffee. Shanks (homemade knives) came out of nowhere, and there I stood with only a year or so left on my sentence trying to be a Christian and knowing that what was about to unfold was not going to be an example of my new-found faith and, in fact, would very likely lead to the remainder of my sentence being extended.

I looked over at my black buddy and saw him begin to huddle with his own and remember feeling so disheartened that he sided with color instead of right and wrong. I have never been one to care about the color of a man's skin, so for me it was hard to watch someone turn his back on me because he needed to be true to his race. I then turned and saw Mike and the other three guys begin to scramble for weapons of some sort, grabbing anything they could find. My bunk bed was one of the few in the dorm that was constructed of metal, and the posts that separated the bottom bunk from the top were actually four metal pipes each measuring about two feet in length. I had never really noticed it before that night until Denny, one of the few stand-up guys in our group, grabbed one end of my bed and started trying to pull the pipe out. I then figured out what he was doing and so did Mike and the others.

The two others joined Mike and Denny and began trying to grab a leg but could not get the top bunk to separate. I remember looking at them and then glancing over at my black friend on the other side. The moment of decision was on me. My friend had already made his, so I was forced to make mine. I ran over to the bed and got under the top bunk on my hands and knees and arched my back up and pushed the whole bed up, releasing the pressure on the posts, while all four guys grabbed one. I then reared up and threw it off my back, and realized all of the sudden that I was the only one without a weapon.

You can only imagine how I was feeling at that point. The dormitory housed around 200 men and the ratio was about 60% black to 40% white. The majority of the blacks were coming our way ready for battle, while all the other whites except us four were on their beds wishing they were anywhere else. And there I stood with nothing in my hand but air.

Well, the moment we started advancing towards each other the doors burst open and the SWAT team came barreling in. I guess when they pulled Little Red and the other boy out of the dorm they probably began gearing up figuring that it would escalate. To be honest with you, I was glad to see them come in and not just because we were outnumbered 25 to 1, but because something like this would have surely extended my stay. I wanted so badly to be free and live the new life that I had found, and I knew that a riot would sabotage that and cost me my parole date.

The Lord truly covered me that night. Things turned out OK. They ended up putting the four of us in holding cells for a few days until things simmered down and then released us back into population. That was my last skirmish in prison. I spent my last year and a half learning how to lay bricks, which was one of the few trades they offered at Buford, and spent the remainder of my time in the Word, lifting weights, and doing anything else I could find that was positive and productive.

A Farewell to Bars: Leaving Prison

I left Buford State Penitentiary in 1988 a much better man than I was when I got there. I went to live with my mom and dad in Fayetteville, Georgia, and took a job with a masonry company in Griffin. My dad helped me get an old truck, and before long I started my own business, Barrow's Masonry, which has been in operation now for over 22 years. God has truly blessed me and many others through that business. I soon became active in AA and NA thinking that this would be a good place for me to meet people who were trying to start a new life without drugs or alcohol. I knew what AA believed and did not agree with their "once an alcoholic always an alcoholic" position nor that you could make your "higher power" a grapefruit if you so choose. But it was a safer bet for me than risking getting back with the old playmates and playgrounds again. I had already found out the hard way that hanging around people who were not the "real deal" could cost me. Here is one such example.

Over the years I had kept in touch with a guy named Milton I did time with in Jackson and I knew that he was doing well, so I gave him a buzz when I got out and went over to his house. He had beat me out by a year or so and had already gotten married, landed a good job, bought a house, and had two late-model cars. I went to see him the day after my release—a day I will never forget. We were sitting out on his back patio talking when suddenly his dog came up with something black in his mouth. Milton reached down and grabbed it out of his dog's mouth and saw that it was a wallet. He opened the wallet and looked at the driver's license and realized that it was his next door neighbor's. He then thumbed through it and discovered a small amount of cash and a few credit cards. How that dog ended up with that wallet we will never know. At this point I looked at Milton and said something to the effect that "I know that you are going to take that and give it back to its rightful owner." He assured me that he would. So I forgot about it and we moved on.

Later that day Milton asked me if I wanted to go with him to look at some stereo equipment that he was thinking about buying to put in his already souped up truck. I said sure and we headed out. When we got to the store Milton began asking for all kinds of speakers, amps, subwoofers, etc. While he was talking with the clerk I started looking at other stuff and drifted away for a moment. Well, I went back over to him just as the clerk was ringing up a truck load of stereo equipment. I then watched Milton pull out the wallet that the dog had brought up on the porch and hand the clerk his next door neighbor's credit card.

Well, at that point I wanted to hit him right upside the head with a strong right and probably would have but for the fact that we were in public and I knew nobody in the world would believe that I knew nothing about what he was doing. I had literally been out of prison for less than 48 hours and my prior record of robbing stores and stealing was as long as I was tall. I remember looking up and seeing that they had a surveillance camera pointed directly at us and the cash register. I looked over and gave Milton a very hard stare that said it all and told him I was leaving. I walked out of the building and started walking home. A few minutes later he pulled up beside me, apologizing and telling me he was sorry so and so on. I hopped in and let him give me a ride home. For some reason nothing ever came of that incident.

Spiritual Warfare: The Believer's Reality

The point to be made here is this: "Don't ever think for one moment that there is not a spiritual battle going on around us all the time." What are the odds of a dog bringing home a wallet full of cash and credit cards and dropping it at the feet of two ex-convicts who had both done time for stealing? I have owned a lot of dogs, and I have never been able to get one to fetch a stick much less my neighbor's wallet. I mean who needs to steal when you have a dog that will pillage the neighborhood for you, right?

The Apostle Paul in Ephesians 6:10-12 (NLT) said: "A final word: Be strong in the Lord and in his mighty power. Put on all of God's armor so that you will be able to stand firm against all *strategies* of the devil. For we are not fighting against flesh-and-blood enemies, but against evil rulers and authorities of the unseen world, against mighty powers in this dark world, and against evil spirits in the heavenly places." Listen, it was no coincidence that situation took place the way it did. The same evil spirits that Paul was talking about back then are the same ones that exist today. It was not the flesh-and-blood Milton that I should have been so mad at but the evil spirit that Milton had allowed to take up residence in his life. You see, those same evil spirits run rampant in the world today doing their best to cause harm to you and to me. They bring stuff right under your nose and try to get you to buy in one more time.

You don't have to be an unbeliever to be tripped up by an evil spirit. As a matter of fact the ones that Satan goes after most often are new converts who have just recently decided to plant themselves in the body of believers. *Why?* Because, like a tree, if you can kill it off before it takes root then you will not have to worry about it once it is full grown. It is much easier to kill a twig than it is to cut down a full grown tree.

We need to be on guard at all times especially as we are starting our Christian walk. That's why the Bible says that the devil comes as a wolf dressed in sheep's clothing prowling around for whom he may devour. I once had a drill sergeant tell me, "Private Barrow, you stay alert, you stay alive." I think about that one quite often and quote it to the men in our ministry on occasion. The fact is if we stay alert the enemy has a lot harder time sneaking up on us. I don't know about you but I've had enough surprise attacks to last me a lifetime.

Settling for the Good vs. God's Best

After being out for a few weeks I met a girl named Dana at an AA meeting and we soon married. She, like me, was just getting her spiritual legs underneath her and, also like me, she had gotten off to a very rough start in life. Her biological father was actually the one who got her started using crystal meth intravenously. Talk about being dealt a bad hand. He had passed away a few years before we met from drug abuse. We stayed married for about a year and it was a very rocky road, to say the least. Although I loved her I soon realized that I had made a big mistake. I had jumped too fast. My old thought pattern that a wife was a safety net had turned around and bitten me. It wasn't long before I slipped and started drinking. I wasn't doing drugs, but drinking was just as bad for me. My relationship with Dana had unraveled because we were two new converts with life-controlling issues trying to get on our feet at the same time. It was a classic case of the blind trying to lead the blind. As I said earlier, unless we learn to walk on our own we will not be able to lead anybody else.

I had not lived in the free world as a clean and sober individual since I first started using at the age of 12. So how could I to teach Dana when I still needed teaching myself? That's why in Teen Challenge, as well as the ministry I run, we frown on men getting into a relationship soon after graduation. They can get involved in something too soon and begin to lose focus on the main relationship—*their relationship with God.* That's exactly what happened to me and what has happened to many other men and women. We stop looking vertically—up—and begin to look horizontally—around us. It is not that we don't still love God—we do. It's just that we get pulled into something that consumes our immediate attention and before we know it we are in too deep. This is especially so when the other person has a lot of her or his own baggage to deal with. That's why it is so important for us not to be unequally yoked in marriage and to wait on God to send us the right life partner.

When the men I minister to ask me about getting into relationships I will usually advise them to take it *very, very slowly.* They will look at me and say, "But, Brother John, she is a good girl and I believe God sent her to me." Well that may be, but always remember that *good* is the number one enemy of *great.* You may settle for good when great is just around the corner. In my life I have found that more often than not it takes great some time to arrive. Listen to what King Solomon said in Proverbs 6:6-8 (NIV): "Go to the ant; consider its ways and be wise! It has no commander, no overseer or ruler, yet it stores its provisions in summer and gathers its food at harvest."

Self-discipline is the ability to voluntarily forego gratification in the present so as to maximize it in the future.

What do you want in the future that will require a sacrifice in the present? We must learn to be patient and give God time to move on our behalf. God is not a checker player. He doesn't play give away, jumping backwards, flying kings, and the like. He plays chess. He's always setting up the board in our lives, positioning things to work out best for us, slowly, methodically, strategically positioning things so that we will come out on top. He doesn't move quickly. It takes time to bring the great things around and put our adversary the devil in checkmate. God is sovereign. He is always orchestrating a series of events in the life of every believer to advance him forward. As the Bible says, Jesus came "to give us life and life more abundantly." Not just life but *abundant* life—more than we could ever hope or ask for. That is the kind of God we serve.

As I said earlier, however, as a new Christian with old mindsets I moved too fast and caused Him to have to reposition the board in my life. This came at a price—costing me time and pain that could have been avoided had I been patient and not accepted the good but waited on the great. My marriage to Dana finally crumbled after about a year when Dana got mad at me and called my parole officer and told him some lies about me. I have always found it hard for a man—especially a man with a prison record—to defend himself against a woman in tears. And my parole officer, who was known to be a hard man, revoked my parole and sent me back to prison for a year. As so often happens, Dana regretted her rash act and begged for my release, but it was too late. Despite all that, however, that year was one of the best of my life.

CHAPTER 6

BUILDING ON THE FOUNDATION

I SPENT THE NEXT 12 months digging into scripture and continuing to build upon my foundation. Although I had made my share of mistakes I was not looking back. I got up, brushed myself off, and went back at it more determined than ever. I filed for a divorce in the prison, asked God to forgive me, and waited on another chance. Some years later Dana was hit by a train and killed. She and a friend were walking on a train trestle, and as the train approached they stepped back behind the steel I-beams of the bridge. Dana made the mistake of poking her head out to see if the train was almost finished coming by when she did a mirror protruding from the train struck her in the head and broke her neck instantly.

I went to the funeral home to see her and recall looking at her young face and thinking how sad it was that she never found peace on this side of eternity. I do believe that she was saved, however, because many times I had seen her praying to God and weeping before His feet. She was another beautiful person who had been dealt a tough hand early on and never got a better one. I suppose that in some cases, like Dana's, the grace of God gives us an early release from a ball and chain that we just can't shake on our own.

Upon my release I went back to my mom and dad's and picked right back up where I had left off with my masonry business. This time I had some money left over from before the parole violation that helped me get going quicker. It was almost as though I had taken a year to go back to seminary. I was ready to go.

Finding God's Best for My Life

Not long after my final release from prison I met Lindsey, who is now my wife of 22 years. I can honestly say that "great" finally arrived. I had tried marriage three times before and failed miserably each time. The Lord obviously saved the best for last. Although Lindsey, unlike me, hadn't left a trail of bad choices behind her she had experimented with drugs in her youth and was very understanding of my past, which really surprised me at the time. Her parents were another matter altogether. We had to break them in slowly over time by dropping subtle hints here and there until one day they just asked about my past. Even then I gave them the watered-down version.

Now nobody in his right mind would want his daughter to marry a man with my record. As the father of a six-year-old daughter now, I understand that more than ever before. It is often difficult to convince people of our heart to change. We can tell them our intentions and try to assure them, but the only way to really prove it is to allow them to see us get up every day, every week, every month, every year and do the next right thing. It is a process that takes time and all we can do is hope they are willing to give it.

But oh how sweet it is when people finally begin to believe in you, and not only believe in you but seek you out for help or advice. Lindsey and I soon joined a local church and served there for the next four years. The Lord continued to bless the work of my hands as my masonry business continued to grow. I was not only able to buy us a house, cars, and everything else we needed but was able to give away a lot to people in need. It seemed that the more money I gave to the church and others in need, the more God would give me back. Within two years our home was paid for, our cars were paid for, and we had money in savings.

It was as if I had walked into a dream. Everything was so sweet in those days. Even though I was street savvy, I was so green to the things of God and the church. It was as if every day were Christmas that presented me with a new beauty to behold. I began to see things that I had never noticed before—sunrises, sunsets, the changing of the leaves in the fall, the blooming of the flowers in the spring, the beauty of the ocean, and so much more. The very things that I used to think were boring became the most precious things in my life. The church, friends, relationships, creation, smelling the grass after I cut it, going to get pumpkins in the fall, a Christmas tree at Christmas. The simple things in life became more than enough for me. Every day I would get up at 4:30 a.m. and do my devotion and pinch myself to see if this was real. I was finally living the life that for so long I had viewed from afar, and it was more than I could have ever expected. God had surely given me the desires of my heart.

Restoring the Years the Locust Ate Away

My grandmother (my dad's mom) was the person who prayed for me most over the years. While I was in prison she once told me: "John, the Bible says in Joel 2:25 that 'I will restore to you the years that the locust have eaten away,' and God is telling me that that is what he is going to do for you one day." I always remembered her telling me that, and I would often reflect on that verse during those honeymoon years as a new believer. What she spoke and believed God for was now coming to pass—for God had surely delivered me out of my bondage and was definitely restoring to me those lost years.

My grandmom is now 92 years old and God let her live to see His promise fulfilled. She is a sweet old saint with a full head of grey hair. Her eyesight is not what it used to be, but her mind is still sharp as a tack. She comes and spends the night with us on occasion and we recall her prayers for me when I was living the life of a prodigal. She is the only one in the family who has had unwavering faith and never let go of God's promises for me. She would actually take my name every time she would go to Jerusalem, put it on a piece of paper and stick it in the Wailing Wall

Grandmother helping
John preach a sermon

At the Jordan River
in Jerusalem

At the
Wailing Wall
in Jerusalem

alongside the hundreds of thousands of others that are stuffed in every crevice in that sacred structure. She spoke of that as well when I was a young man. She would tell me that my name was in the Holy Land and that God was going to remember His promises to her. At that time I thought, "OK, Grandmom, sure thing," not even really understanding what the Wailing Wall was.

Sometime later I did, though. A few years back we took a trip to Jerusalem and visited the Wailing Wall. I stood at a distance and gazed at all those massive stones that King Solomon and his mighty army erected with countless scraps of white paper shoved into every crook and crevice. I will never forget (and can hardly express) the feelings that flooded my heart when I realized that somewhere among them all was my name—my very own name—because more than three decades earlier a woman who believed in her God so much had stood there praying for a boy some 6,000 miles away who was so lost. I was blown away by that experience, through which God revealed another layer of His goodness to me. That day I knelt before the same Wailing Wall that she had knelt before and not only praised Him for His faithfulness, but put my grandmother's name in there as she had mine. I thanked God for her prayers and asked Him to heal her eyes and to give her continued strength and vitality until that day. That was a milestone in my life that I will never forget.

Back to Prison ... as a Chaplain

As time passed the Department of Corrections granted me approval to go back inside the prisons as a volunteer chaplain. I even had my own ID card. Talk about a miracle. I began going into Macon Correctional Institution, Jackson, Milledgeville, Buford, county camps, jails, juvenile detention centers, and many others. I also went in with Bill Glass Ministries on quite a few occasions. One of the most interesting places I ever visited was Angola State Penitentiary in Louisiana. At one time Angola was known as the bloodiest prison in the United States of America. Angola is so famous amongst prisons that they even have a museum of sorts right outside the gate where all kinds of homemade weapons that

At Angola State Prison

Mural of Daniel in the Lions Den – Death Chamber of Angola St. Prison

were confiscated from inmates over the years are on display. There are pictures and articles of all the murders and attempted escapes that took place over the years. Angola was a very brutal place and is very well known in the prison world today.

Although I had been in some pretty rough prisons and endured some rather harsh situations inside, visiting Angola made me realize that it can *always* be worse. Much worse. You have heard the old saying, "It's the end of the road for you." Well, Angola is truly that—the end of the road. When you arrive at Angola the last road you turn on is a very long one—stretching quite a few miles. You just keep driving for what seems like forever on this flat, barren, deserted-looking road before finally you start seeing this little dot straight ahead of you. And as you get closer and closer you begin to see these big ominous looking gates that resemble the gates to hell itself. The prison is literally where the road ends, and you can only imagine what it must feel like when you arrive as an inmate on a bus. It is definitely not a place that any sane person would put on his bucket list.

Upon our arrival at Angola we were searched and ID'd and then escorted to the place we would be staying for the next three days. The two guys who were with me were both ex-cons whom the Lord had redeemed as well. We felt like Shadrach, Meshach, and Abednego heading into the fiery furnace with an opportunity to testify to the delivering power of the One we serve. I don't know that I have ever had a richer opportunity for evangelism than I had at Angola. As I said earlier, Angola was once known as the bloodiest prison in the United States of America. Today, however, Angola is regarded as one of the safest prisons in America. Let me explain. When Angola was at its peak of brutality in 1995, a new warden was brought in to see if he could bring about change. His name was Burl Cain. No warden had ever made it over seven years at Angola. Most lasted only four or five before being fired for not being able to control the violence. Burl Cain is still there today some 18 years later. The difference between Burl and the others was this: Burl just so happened to be a born-again Christian who realized that the only way to help reform a man was by changing his heart. No other warden had ever taken that approach and no other warden had ever succeeded.

Angola has over 5,100 inmates, 3,700 of whom are lifers. The average sentence of an Angola inmate is 93 years, meaning that the over 90% will die there. Given this degree of hopelessness you can see the reason for the unbridled violence. Burl Cain understood this as well and thus began to do something different. He reached out to the ministries of Mike Barber, Chuck Colson, Franklin Graham, and many other smaller ministries, such as us three, and sought God's wisdom to help him and the others know how and what to do to penetrate the hearts of these hopeless individuals. Well, it wasn't long before the Lord gave Warden Cain and his team a plan.

It went like this: Angola is on an 18,000-acre plot of land surrounded by the Mississippi River. Given the swamps, rattlesnakes, and alligators escape attempts are few. The inmates at Angola work many different jobs, most of them out in the fields planting and harvesting all kinds of fruits, vegetables, cotton, and other crops. And being such a large place with a huge population the men are housed in many different dormitories. Warden Cain soon realized that he had to begin the process of change one dormitory at a time. He thought to himself that if he could just get a few men in that dorm to truly commit to the God he served, disciple them well, give them jobs as dorm pastors instead of field workers, then maybe, just maybe, with the Lord's help, those few could begin to help change the others and therefore begin to do the same thing in every other dorm on the campus. The plan began to work. One by one each group began to change from the inside out and Warden Cain soon had a prison full of pastors and born-again inmates.

Once these men began to feel and experience the love of God and realize that the life sentence they had received here on earth did not in any way dictate their eternal life sentence that all receive in the future, they began to view things in a different way. They began to understand what the Apostle Peter meant when he wrote that "we are aliens and strangers in this world and this world is not our home." After experiencing grace, love, mercy, forgiveness, and a new perspective on life and eternity, these men began to change, and within a few years life at Angola was much different from before.

By the time I visited Angola there was not only a Bible college but numerous large churches pastored by inmates that held services every night of the week. One inmate pastor even turned down a parole date because he knew that God wanted him to finish his race shepherding the flock that he had grown to love so dearly inside those walls. Talk about being the real deal. There were also pastors who were assigned to minister to the dying men on death row as well as their families. They even had a hospice and a hospice pastor to minister to the many dying men who were coming to the end of their journey. I will never forget kneeling beside a fairly young man who was dying with cancer and sensing how ready he was to meet the Lord. There was no fear in him at all. He certainly ministered to me as much as I ministered to him.

We just so happened to be at Angola when they were having their annual rodeo that actually airs on ESPN. What a great experience that rodeo was. I sat just across from Harry Connick, Jr. As the rodeo began several big white horses came galloping out with inmates riding them carrying banners emblazoned with such messages as "King of Kings," "Lord of Lords," "Jehovah," and the like. A large group of inmates held hands and formed a prayer circle around the center of the ring. One of the crazy things they did was tie $250 to the head of a bull and allow a few of the inmates to try to grab it. That's a lot of money to most of the men in Angola. That bull threw some of them in the air as if they were paper dolls. It was quite a sight to behold.

On the last day at Angola we visited the death chamber where they actually administer the lethal injections to kill the men on death row. I will always remember walking into the room where the condemned men eat their last meal before being put to death. A huge mural on the wall featured Daniel sitting in the middle of the lion's den. The painting was so vivid, so real, that I could envision a condemned man sitting there taking his last meal looking at that painting and hoping and praying that the same God who delivered Daniel might deliver him as well in that final hour. I recall thinking how good God had been to me in sparing my life and not repaying me an eye for an eye and a tooth for a tooth as my sins deserved. I realized how very easily I could have been in the same boat as some of these condemned men if I had only made a tragic decision while in a drugged state or drunken stupor. I recall being so moved and so grateful for all that God had brought me through.

That trip to Angola will be in my mind and heart forever. It turned out like a lot of mission trips to impoverished countries do: You go with the intention of ministering to them only to walk away being ministered to. Praise God for all His tender mercies.

Answering the Call: Remember Ministries

After doing prison ministry for quite a few years and getting involved with ex-offenders, I started a ministry with a dear friend of mine named Buck Scoggins. We named it Remember Ministries. It was named

"Remember" because Buck and I knew the importance of remembering where we had been as well as what God had so mercifully delivered us from. It was also a "call" to anyone who would listen, to remember the Lord as He told the disciples at His last supper when he broke the bread and gave it to His disciples on the night He was betrayed: "this do in remembrance of me" (Luke 22:19). It was very important to Jesus that His friends look back

Buck Scoggins of "Remember" Ministries

and reflect on what they had seen during their three-year

journey with Him as well as what they were about to see during the coming 24 hours—His crucifixion. We, like His first disciples, need always to look back to be reminded of what He taught us when we were closest to Him.

It had always been a challenge for me to stop and look back when I was in the middle of *doing* life. Looking back is not always easy when you are caught up in the middle of the moment. Looking back is a learned behavior that comes over time with effort and discernment. Looking back is vital at those times when you begin to falter or doubt and you hear the voice of the Holy Spirit begin to speak softly, saying "hold steady, son, remember, remember me, remember when I spoke to you, touched you, delivered you, healed you. Let's downshift here and look back. Remember, son, remember your day of visitation." That moment might have come during a worship song, a morning devotion, a church service, or the week after your failure. It was that precious moment when you felt the peace of God that surpasses all understanding rest upon your shoulder and whisper in your ear, "I love you. It's going to be all right. I am here to help you. I will never leave you nor forsake you. You are not what the world and Satan say you are. You are My son or daughter, and we are going to get this flat spot in your wheel fixed once and for all."

It is so important for believers to begin to practice looking back to those sweet moments of intimacy and deliverance. Reflection has a way of keeping you grounded. It has a way of stabilizing your walk with God and helping you not to buy into the devil-inspired myth that the "grass is always greener on the other side of the fence." As I tell myself and the men I minister to: "The reason that the grass is greener over there is that there is a whole lot of !@#$ over there. It makes great fertilizer."

Remember Ministries began to meet on a monthly basis, and I bought an old home and remodeled it to provide a place for ex-offenders to stay after being paroled. The Department of Corrections approved the place as a home that inmates could parole to. We never had more than six or so guys there at a time, and I was not heavily involved at the residence. It was really more of a transition home for Christian men who needed a place to stay long enough to get on their feet. It was very different from the ministry that I run now. I kept the home running for a while and with God's blessing we were able to get quite a few men back on their feet. I eventually sold the home and headed in another direction due to a change of season in my life.

Buck Scoggins: The Art of Finishing Well

We continued going into prisons and Buck pushed the Remember meaning and logo until his dying day. He hung up banners, made billboards, set out yard signs, and put stickers on as many cars as people would allow. If you drive through Spalding County, Georgia, you will surely see them. Buck died at 82 years after serving the Lord for almost 50 years. He had started off on the wrong foot but finished on the right one. Buck, like a lot of other men in prison, was an underdog from the start. He was born in Cabbage Town back in 1930. He had no father figure around. He was raised by a single mom and by the streets of Atlanta. He made the journey that many prodigals make—juvenile detention, jail, prison. Buck served a lot of time in two of Georgia's toughest prisons back then—Reidsville and the Atlanta Federal Pen. He was known as one of Georgia's most incorrigible inmates. After Buck endured many hard knocks and many long stints in solitary confinement, a prison guard befriended him and gave him a Bible to read. A short time later Buck asked the Lord to change him—and that He did.

Buck not only got saved but made parole and never returned to prison. He went on to graduate from Bible college and became an ordained minister. A changed man indeed, Buck spent the rest of his life serving God and going back to prisons preaching the delivering power of Jesus Christ. When he died he didn't even have enough money to pay his electric bill. They found him in his house in sweltering heat well over 90 degrees, and Buck had never asked me or anybody else to help him with the bill.

A few weeks before he died, Buck called seeking help to make more Remember stickers. That's where his heart was. He knew that this old earth was not his home. Buck Scoggins was a dear friend and a true example of what happens to a man when he truly sells out to his God. It was an honor for me to conduct his funeral and not have to search for kind words to say. I could have talked for hours and never run out of stories to tell about all of the great things Buck had done. All because Buck sat down with God one day in the locker room of life and decided to come out and give it all he had in the second half. I thought it was just like God to allow Buck to marry my wife and me some 20 years ago and now to allow me to bury him. Only God could do that. Here is a poem by Myra B. Welch that I read at Buck's funeral. It describes so well my dear friend Buck, me, and many of you reading this book right now.

The Touch of the Master's Hand

Twas battered and scarred, and the auctioneer
thought it scarcely worth his while
To waste much time on the old violin,
But held it up with a smile.

"What am I bidden, good folks," he cried,
"Who'll start the bidding for me?
A dollar, a dollar, then, two! Only two?
Two dollars, and who'll make it three?

Three dollars, once; three dollars, twice;
Going for three ..."
But no,

From the room, far back, a grey-haired man
Came forward and picked up the bow;
Then, wiping the dust from the old violin,
And tightening the loose strings,
He played a melody pure and sweet
As a caroling angel sings.

The music ceased, and the auctioneer,
With a voice that was quiet and low, said:

"What am I bid for the old violin?"
And he held it up with the bow.

"A thousand dollars, and who'll make it two?
"Two thousand! And who'll make it three?
"Three thousand, once; three thousand, twice;
And going and gone," said he.

The people cheered, but some of them cried,
"We do not quite understand, what changed its worth?"
Swift came the reply:
"The Touch Of The Master's Hand."

And many a man with life out of tune,
And battered and scarred with sin,
Is auctioned cheap to the thoughtless crowd,
Much like the old violin.

A 'mess of potage,' a glass of wine;

A game—and he travels on.
He is 'going' once, and 'going' twice,
He's 'going' and almost 'gone.'

But the Master comes and the foolish crowd
Never can quite understand
The worth of a soul and the change that's wrought
By the touch of the Master's Hand.

I will always *Remember* my friend Buck and look forward to our reunion one day. I am confident that he is just as committed in the kingdom as he was here on earth. My guess is that the pearly gates are now covered with Remember stickers and that there are billboards lining all the streets of gold.

It's Never Too Late: Finding Your Special Place to Serve

Well some of you may be saying, "It's too late for me. I am too old, too stuck in my ways, and I've made way too many bad choices...." Listen, think for a minute about the thief on the cross beside Jesus. He asked Jesus to forgive him in his final hour and Jesus told him: "Today you will be with me in paradise." It is *never* too late to join "team Jesus"—the only team in history that can *promise* you a championship—*the* championship of the ages! Jesus told a great story for people like you (Mathew 20:1-16):

> "God's kingdom is like an estate manager who went out early in the morning to hire workers for his vineyard. They agreed on a wage of a dollar a day, and went to work. Later, about nine o'clock, the manager saw some other men hanging around the town square unemployed. He told them to go to work in his vineyard and he would pay them a fair wage. They went. "He did the same thing at noon, and again at three o'clock. At five o'clock he went back and found still others standing around. He said, 'Why are you standing around all day doing nothing?' They said, 'Because no one hired us.' He told them to go to work in his vineyard. When the day's work was over, the owner of the vineyard instructed his foreman, 'Call the workers in and pay them their wages. Start with the last hired and go on to the first.' Those hired at five o'clock came up and were each given a dollar. When those who were hired first saw that, they assumed they would get far more. But they got the same, each of them one dollar. Taking the dollar, they groused angrily to the manager, 'These last workers put in only one easy hour, and you just made them equal to us, who slaved all day under a scorching sun.' He replied to the one speaking for the rest, 'Friend, I haven't been unfair. We agreed on the wage of a dollar, didn't we? So take it and go. I decided to give to the one who came last the same as you. Can't I do what I want with my own money? Are you going to get stingy because I am generous?' Many of the first ending up last, and the last first."

You must understand that wherever you are in life you must start right there. Today can be the first day of your new life. God will not look back and remember your failures. As a matter of fact He can't! Buck called me one day laughing on the phone. "John," he said, "did you know that God has amnesia?" I said, "No, Buck, I didn't." He went on to remind me of the scripture that says, "I will cast your sins as far as the east is from the west and I will remember them no more." You see, it doesn't matter how late it is because once you fall to your knees, confess your sins before God, and ask Him to lead you from that day forward, you will be a new creation in Christ Jesus and He will no longer be able to remember your sins even if He wanted to (which He doesn't).

From that day forward, however, we need to be about our Father's business. Revelation 22:12 says: "Look, I am coming soon! My reward is with me, and I will give to each person according to what they have done." At the point of conversion, be reminded that you can not only start counting on your inheritance as a child of God but you also begin to do good works (by His enabling grace and power through you) so that upon His soon return He will have extra rewards for you. A lot of us know what it's like to make a bad investment, whether it is an investment of our time, our money, or our emotions, and to end up wishing that we had not made it. Well, here is an investment tip that we can all rest assured will produce a great and satisfying returns. We will not regret that we picked the wrong door again, and we won't be standing there kicking ourselves saying "how did I miss it again?"

The other day I was talking to a friend who mentioned a person who was dying. After a moment I quietly said, "I am dying also." Well his eyes popped wide open and he said, "What's wrong, John?" I just looked at him for a moment and said, "You're dying, too." Well, he got the point and laughed. You see, it's true, we're all dying. We are all perishable beings, and the more we realize, as King David said, we are but a vapor, the more we will realize that we don't have much time left to work on our heavenly bank account. And what better way to make deposits into that account than to pour out of your well of trials and errors? Many of the men I minister to ask me what I think they should do for God when they graduate. Some ask if they should go to the mission field or something along those lines. My response is: "Serve where you are the most educated."

In the military there are two ranks that carry the same authority yet are different in title: *corporal* and *specialist*. As a corporal you may be trained to do a lot of things without specializing in any. If you are a specialist, however, that means the military has sent you to specialize in one main thing. That is the way it is with ministry, too. You and God will get the most mileage from serving in the place where you have the most experience. For me that is helping men with life-controlling issues such as substance abuse, etc. For you that may be the same or you may be better suited for ministering to mentally handicapped persons, single mothers, sexual abuse survivors, people who are dying (hospice type work), people addicted to gambling, people who struggle with homosexual issue, and the list goes on and on. Know this: Whatever you have had to learn the hard way will surely benefit others and encourage them when they hear you share your experiences and the things you learned going through it. That's why the guy in Angola said, "I think I'll just stay here instead of seek parole because God can get more mileage from me here than He can out there."

I realize that was an extreme move that most of us would not have made. But when your eyes are on the Kingdom and you truly realize that you are dying and that the end is closer than you think, you could possibly make the same decision too. And the truth is that what we are asked to do pales in comparison to what so many of our forefathers in the faith did. Jesus, the very Son of God, was of course flogged, tortured, and crucified. But do you know how His disciples, men just like you and me, finished their race as well?

- Peter was crucified upside down
- Andrew was hung on a cross at Patra
- James was thrown from the top of a temple and beaten to death with a club

CHAPTER 7

EVERYDAY MIRACLES

N OT LONG AFTER Lindsey and I were married we began trying
to have children, but for some reason it just didn't happen. We
spent thousands on infertility doctors, *in vitro* fertilization, and
even checked into surrogacy, but all was to no avail. So we then began to
check into adoption. If you know anything about adoption you know
that unless you have a squeaky clean record you are highly unlikely to
be able to adopt a child.

We visited various adoption agencies, but as soon as they asked me
about my past the meetings would immediately take a downward turn
and they would tell me, "Sir, it is very difficult to get a child placed in a
home when someone has a DUI, much less when they have burglaries,
drug sales, armed robberies, and more. We think it would be a waste of
time to go any further with this." At that point we would walk out and
say, "God, only you can open this door."

At some point I stopped setting up appointments and would just call
and talk with the adoption agencies by phone. I would start the conversation with "Let me tell you this first before we go any further" and then
proceed to tell them about my past. As usual they would say, "We don't
think you have a chance." After doing this for quite some time I would
get discouraged and quit for a while ... until I got inspired again and
would go back at it. One day I called the Lutheran Ministries of Georgia

and spoke to a little Jewish lady named Paula Budnitz. I began the conversation as usual spilling the mess of my past and then asked her if it was a waste of time. To my surprise, she said, "Let me get to know you before we decide that."

Adopting Noah

So Lindsey and I went to her office on Peachtree Street in Atlanta and filled out the paperwork to begin the process. We then went to the Fayette County Sheriff's Office to go get fingerprinted and get a copy of our criminal records. I will never forget that day. We walked up to the counter and addressed the clerk who was separated from us by a sheet of Plexiglass with two holes in it—one for communicating and the other for passing papers and such. The clerk was a really young girl who didn't appear to be a day over 18 and made us wonder if this was her first day on the job. We requested our records, paid the fee, filled out the paperwork, and then stood there and waited for our reports. From where we were standing we could see the machine that printed them out. We watched as the clerk went over and retrieved Lindsey's report first. She pulled it off the printer and came back to us and smiled as she handed us the blank piece of paper that was proof of Lindsey's squeaky clean past.

She then returned to the printer and waited on my report. After a rather lengthy wait (I imagine that even the computer had problems compiling such a magnitude of horror), the printer finally began spitting it out. The young clerk's back was to us while she waited on the report and as it began she would glance over her shoulder and smiled at us every so often as if to say that she was sorry for the slow computer. As my rap sheet began to come out, however, her cute little smile began to fade into something strained like when you pass gas very quietly in the middle of church while you are looking directly at the pastor, and you just smile as if you are hanging on his every word when you are really relieved that it didn't make any noise as you set the captive free. My record went all the way to the floor and began to fold back and forth, back and forth, like an accordion expanding and contracting, and every few minutes the girl

The adoption of Noah

The Barrow Children

would glance over her shoulder with that new smile while Lindsey and I felt like crawling beneath the counter and hiding until it was over.

After what seemed like an eternity she stooped over and collected what looked like something from a paper drive and walked back over to us and fed it through the slot in the window as we just smiled that smile at each other. We thanked her and headed to the car thanking God that was over and wondering who in their right mind would place a child in a home with someone who had done the things I had done. Even though I knew I was not that guy any more, I just couldn't see a birth mother or a judge allowing it to take place.

Paula Budnitz came to our house and spent a good amount of time with us. She talked to my pastor and my other references. She did her research and "due diligence" and in the end concluded that she could endorse me. So she took the case and went to work on our behalf. The way private adoption works is that they do a lengthy bio on you (including your record) and compile a portfolio with pictures, etc. Then they present you and one or two other couples to the birth mother and father (if he is in the picture) to choose from. I figured that it could be a long time, if ever, before a girl would pick us when she had two other families to pick from. I mean think about it: The girl is already questioning whether or not she is making the right decision, so the least she can do is place her child in the safest possible family environment, right? That would be the most logical conclusion, eh? Well, I should have known by then that God doesn't always show up in man's most logical conclusions.

The very first couple we were presented to picked us first, but something happened to the case (I can't recall exactly what) and it didn't work out. So we were presented to another birth mother and again we were picked first this second time as well, and this time worked out! We were notified that we would be getting a little boy as soon as the mother delivered. We would then have to meet at a Fayette County judge's office so he could review the paperwork and put his stamp of approval on the adoption. Now you would think by now that my faith would be as strong and solid as Samson given all that I had seen God do. But to be honest I was still a little anxious about how the judge would rule. They had advised us that he would make the final call. When that day arrived we all assembled in his office—Lindsey, Paula, the judge, Noah (who was hopefully to be our newborn son), and me. The judge glanced through a few papers and then said a few words and it was over. Noah was officially our son.

This was one of those God moments when you know that He had just worked a miracle before your very eyes. The Bible says that He will give you the desires of your heart and He surely did. Noah is now 15 years old, active in church, plays football, goes to a Christian school, and is a great son and friend to both his mother and me. We have been so blessed to help God raise him and to instill in him Godly values and character. Take it from me, it feels so good to be able to use your past mistakes as stepping stones for your children.

Starting a Business

As I said earlier, during my last year and a half at Buford I signed up for masonry school and learned how to lay bricks and stone. I had tried welding first but soon realized that I was not wired to be shut up in a dark room all day wearing heavy leather pants and jacket and a big helmet. I'm glad I switched trades because my masonry company has been "the little train that could" for the last 23 years. When I first started the business I ran an ad in the service guide of the Atlanta Journal-Constitution, passed out flyers, and hung little signs on telephone poles at four-way intersections that read: "Brick, Block, Stone and Tile" and listed my phone number. The city workers would come and take the signs down, so I would go back with a ladder and place the signs up higher so that they couldn't reach them. (Remember that I was a new believer at the time.) They finally ended up calling me at the phone number on the signs and made me come take them down myself. But not before I had gotten quite a bit of work from them.

One of the first jobs I got when I started was to brick a little patio. The lady had all the brick, so all I had to do was get the sand and the mortar.

When I went to meet with her and give her an estimate for the job, I figured the price based on left brain logic and not on industry standards and wisdom. The way I figured it was that this job would take me about three days to complete and at that time I had been used to making about $100 a day. So I thought that if I charged her $600 I would make double what I would have made working for someone else, and that would be great. I turned in my price of $600 and added another $100 or so for sand and mortar. She awarded me the job, and I spent the next few days working like a Trojan. I didn't want to go over my estimated time-frame, which would require me to make another trip from where I was living in Peachtree City up to Alpharetta and would cost me another whole day.

I remember finishing the job late in the evening, well after sunset, and the homeowner had turned on all her backyard lights. I also recall being totally spent and exhausted, which was saying something considering that I was in great shape at the time. After I finished the job, the lady came outside and handed me a check for my work and asked me a question I will never forget. "John," she said, "I just have one question for you: How did you do this job so cheap? The lowest bid I had was around $3,000 and you did it for $600."

Now I may not be the sharpest knife in the drawer, but I sure am good at math. I realized immediately that I had just left at least $2,000 on the table. I mean, even if I had quoted her $2,600 I would have been $400 less than the other guy and would have still gotten the job. So I just looked at her like someone who thought he had won the lottery only to find out that he had misread one of the numbers. I stood there thinking: Should I tell her that I just enjoyed hard labor and working for free? Or, maybe tell her that I thought it was Christmas and just figured that I would be the gift that kept on giving? All I can remember is that I spent that long ride home that night trying to pull my foot out of my butt and thinking about how to avoid making that mistake ever again. And I didn't.

For the next job I estimated, I took pictures, precise measurements, and so on and then started calling other masonry companies in the phone book to ask them what they would charge to do a job with these specs and used their wisdom until I could figure out how to price jobs on my own. I want to note that I did not lie to these companies and tell them that it was my job and I wanted them to do it. I would just ask for their help without adding a bunch of information. Some were more than willing to help me whereas others would hang up on me so as not to help their competition. It took me a year or so to get to the point that I knew just a little. I look back now and realize that I learned a lot at other people's expense. You see, in masonry school all you learn are the fundamentals so that when you get out you are an apprentice at best. It takes a long time working out in the field to know what you are doing.

We Get Better One Brick at a Time

I recall a rather strange experience I had building my first stone mailbox. The client was a little old black lady. I remember going out to her house and seeing iron bars on her windows and doors. (I instantly felt right at home.) When I got there to figure the job she just barely cracked the door and asked me if I would build her a stone mailbox. Of course I said yes. And that was it. No pictures of my past work, no taking me around the neighborhood to point out others that she wanted it to look like, no preference for the color of stone, no checking references, no nothing. She just said, "Build it," and then closed the door. I wondered if maybe there was a reason for those bars on every opening in the house. Maybe they were there to keep out all the bill collectors and everybody else she ripped off. It was really weird to say the least.

Since I figured I didn't have much to lose and wasn't exactly in big demand at the time I built her a mailbox. After I completed the mailbox I went to the door to tell her and ask her to come out and look at it, but all she did was crack the door, hand me a check, and thank me for my services. I asked her if she wanted to come out and inspect it, and she said no. You can probably guess that I went directly to the bank to cash the check, which I would have bet the farm was no good. But it was. I learned a very valuable lesson that day: *Never judge the old book by the cover.*

Years later, after my business was thriving, a call came in one day. I heard this little voice on the other end of the line saying, "Mr. Barrow, you built me a mailbox and one of the stones fell off of it, can you come and put it back on?" When I went out to inspect the situation I realized that it was this little old lady's house. So many years had passed that I had totally forgotten this job, but as I sat there and looked at the mailbox I could hardly believe that I had built it. The stone work was not good at all. It was a wonder I had even gotten paid for it. At the time I did it, however, I truly was proud of my work and thought I had done a great job. Just like most things when we start out, we learn as we go and hope we get better and better over time. So I didn't just replace the loose stone but built her a brand-new mailbox. I don't remember if I even went to the door when I was finished. All I know is that I learned a lot at her house.

Doing the Right Thing: Rendering Unto Caesar What is Caesar's

Back in those days I had no office, no cell phone, no secretary, and no insurance. I had nothing but a small truck, a wheelbarrow, and a few hand tools. I would get paid for a job, cash the check, pay any help that I may have had, and then go on to the next job. It went on like this for a year or two before one day I got to thinking and asked myself, "Aren't you supposed to be paying taxes on some of this money you are making?" I had been so glad that I was not drinking, drugging, or doing anything stupid that paying taxes never even crossed my mind. So I began searching for a CPA who could help me straighten things out. I told him that I hadn't been paying any taxes and needed to start as well as pay any back taxes I owed for the last year or so. I told him that I had a bunch of cash stored up and part of it was Uncle Sam's.

The CPA just looked at me as though he couldn't believe what had just come out of my mouth—as if to say: *So you have a bunch of untraceable cash and you want to give it to the government?* I told him that I didn't want to keep anything that wasn't rightfully mine and that I wanted him to get what I owed to the government. This man did my taxes for 15 years or so and he told that story over and over. Now that I understand more about the injustice of the system I know why it seemed so crazy, but back then I didn't know anything about all that. I am glad I didn't because I don't know if I would have been so generous. As it turned out, I ended up putting around $100,000 in my checking account so that I could give Uncle Sam his cut.

The Blessing of Forgiving Betrayal

Barrows Masonry began to really take off. I began advertising in the *Yellow Pages*, got incorporated, and began to run a legitimate business. God was giving me more than I could have ever imagined. At this time I happened upon another blessing that I hadn't even seen coming. A close friend and his wife used to go out to eat and see a movie with Lindsey and me on Saturday nights. They would always order chicken or hamburgers off the menu while Lindsey and I ordered steak or seafood. So one night I asked him why they didn't get a steak or something, and he told me that on his salary he couldn't afford it. So I just got in the habit of picking up their dinner check, but at the same time I wished there was a way that I could help him rise above his situation.

One night at dinner as we were talking I got an idea. Back then I used to mail out flyers advertising our masonry services as another way of marketing. I suggested that the next time I did a flyer mail-out, I would have some extras printed so that he could go out and bid some of the jobs when he got off work from his regular job. I figured that might help him out. Well as it turned out, it worked very well. He would go out, meet with the customer, take pictures, pull measurements, and bring all the information back to me. I would take the information he had gathered and figure the estimate for the job and he would turn it in. Before long he had quite a few jobs and was making more in the evenings than at his day job. So he quit and started working full-time for me.

He ended up working for me for years until one day I opened up the *Yellow Pages* and right there beside my ad was his ad. He had gone out and started his own business without even discussing it with me. The very guy I had tried to help because I loved him had not even shown me the respect of sitting down with me and talking to me first. I will never forget opening that book and seeing his ad there. It wasn't as much about gaining competition as it was about losing a friend. His betrayal really hurt me because I had mailed out those flyers with one thing in mind—helping him. My wife Lindsey had told me that she could tell that his wife had grown jealous of my success, and we both knew that for a long time she had been whispering in his ear to leave. When I confronted him about it, he said the reason he didn't tell me first was that he was scared and didn't know how. That may very well have been true, but it is important to handle things the right way or they can stink up a place real quick.

I often counsel the men I minister to as well as my own children that "it's not so much *what* you do as *how* you do it." If he had come to me and sat down and discussed his plans to launch his own venture with the outcome would have been much better. Would it have still bothered me? Yes, because I considered him not just an employee, but a friend, and he was making three times the money he used to make. *Money*.

Money is a very dangerous thing. Jesus had more to say about money than any other subject except for the Kingdom. The fact that He spoke so much about it shows us that it was a major topic in His eyes. He knew that it had the power to damage—if not destroy—relationships and that people would lie, cheat, steal, and do a multitude of other things to acquire it. The Bible says that the love of money is the root of all evil (1 Timothy 6:10). That is one of the reasons that the men in our ministry are not allowed to have money for the first year. This prevents them from having to face that hurdle until they can get the other ones worked out.

As I was down and discouragement about my friend's betrayal the Lord reminded me just how many times in my past I had not been faithful to Him. He also showed me the many blessings He had bestowed on my business in large part because of my outstretched hand. By the time my friend finally quit I had other salesmen doing the same thing he had done. It had worked out so well with him that I had used it as a business model with many others. What had begun as my effort to help him turned out not only helping him but helping me even more. The business had grown to the point that we were grossing over $3,000,000 a year with about a 30% profit margin. I couldn't complain about anything. All I could say was "Thank You, Lord for all that You have done."

Blessed Adventures: Hearing and Seeing God in His Creation

Lindsey and I began to travel a good bit back in those days—"a good bit" back then meant two to three weeks a year. A good bit now would mean two to three *months* a year. Back then if I were gone more than a few weeks I would have to unravel a mess of problems on jobs when I returned. Now I have people who can run it for me while I'm gone. Those years are what I refer to as our "honeymoon years." We would take off for various exotic islands such as Aruba, Bermuda, Grand Cayman, Barbados, St. Thomas, St. John, and others. We loved to go on cruises and usually went on at least one or two a year. My favorite part of a cruise was getting up early while the stars were still out and waiting on the sun to rise. Something very special takes place as you view the sun rising over the vast blue water in that pre-dawn hour. The Lord speaks His loudest through His creation. Nothing ministers to me any better than that.

I have been a morning person since I developed the habit in prison. Early morning has become a very special time for me and I wouldn't trade it for anything. Mornings are so sacred. King David said in the Psalms, "Early will I seek you." The Bible refers again and again to Jesus' rising before daybreak. Another point to remember about this time of day is that Satan was known before his rebellion as "the son of the morning." We must ask *why*. Why was Satan given such a name? Well at that time Satan was God's right-hand Angel—His second in command. Having a title that referred to you as "the morning" suggests that the morning was very special to God. You see, Jesus is also known as "the

Bright and Morning Star." Have you ever noticed morning stars? I just now came in from outside my house. It's around 5:30 a.m. The beautiful clear sky this morning is sparkling with brilliant stars. As I gaze at the stars in the sky I always get a great sense of peace in my soul and can hear the Father say to me, "I love you, John. Nothing that comes your way today is too big for us to handle. Just keep walking with your head and your heart up here and with your body and your feet down there and everything is going to be all right. I have great things in store for you when you get home. It won't be long and we'll all be together up here. That day will come sooner than you think, Son. Have a great day today and remember that I am by your side as you go through it." Mornings are so precious—the very best time of the day.

Although Lindsey and I loved the water so much that we both got certified in scuba diving, I was the one who ended up really loving it. I even bought underwater metal detectors, rented boats, got a GPS, and went treasure hunting in the Florida Keys. I bought books that give you the grid coordinates of old sunken ships on the bottom of the ocean. I bought spear guns and had a blast shooting grouper, snapper, and all kinds of great eating fish. This got me in a little trouble one day, however.

I had been out of prison for around six years or so and hadn't been in any trouble with the law except for a speeding ticket or two. I considered myself redeemed, reformed, and renewed. One day, however, while vacationing down in Key West with a friend, we decided to swim out into the harbor to do some spear fishing in the hopes of catching dinner. We were staying at a resort on the waterfront so we didn't have to get on a boat. We could actually see our wives by the pool from where we were and the depth of the water was only about 25-30 feet.

When we dropped down to the ocean floor, however, we were amazed to discover all kinds of old relics from ships that had anchored there over the years. We found some very old bottles, forks and spoons, and a lot of other neat things. I later learned that the reason a lot of that stuff was still out there was that the locals didn't dive that site too much because it was notorious for sharks, who liked to come in and eat what the people threw overboard as they anchored and vacationed in the harbor. (Great info to get *after* the fact!)

I'm glad we did our dive at midday rather than during dinner hour. I had seen quite a few sharks on past dives, but none had ever come towards me. I knew a sure way to keep from getting attacked if they did, though, but I usually kept that secret to myself. It was an old trick I learned in prison that I didn't share with too many people, especially my fellow divers. "Never dive alone" is a golden rule in the diving world because if you get in trouble your partner very likely will save your life. The silver rule might be "always carry a knife" so that if you get tangled in sea weed or a net you can cut yourself free. It's also good to have on hand for protection. Most divers keep their knives in a sheath on their leg or shoulder. I kept mine on my shoulder for a quicker retrieval. Both the knife and the dive partner are essential for this anti-shark-attack strategy to work.

Here's how it works: *When the shark approaches and begins circling you, and you and your partner realize that it is about to attack, you just draw your knife very quickly, slash your partner across his upper torso, and then swim off as fast as you can. Works every time.*☺ Sounds like some Christians I've met along the way.

The $1,000 Lobster Dinner and a Trip to Jail

Back to the story. After we got comfortable on our dive and built a pile of old treasures to come back and get when we had a bigger bag, we began spearing some grouper. Not knowing that we were in a shark-infested area I proceeded to cut the heads off the grouper and gutted them under the water and placed them in the net bag tied around my waist. What a day, we thought, as we spotted lobster scurrying around the place. I grabbed them, broke off their heads (Florida lobsters have no claws), and then put the tails in the bag with the cleaned grouper. Before long the bag got full so I handed it to my buddy to carry while I continued scavenging. Unlike me he was not an avid diver and was not certified. I was the one doing all the hunting and yet having to keep a close eye on him at the same time.

It was then that he did something all new divers tend to do. He floated up to the surface to look around and get a better bearing on his location. I watched him ascend and knew what he was doing—putting his mind at ease. But when he got to the top I saw him drop the bag with all the fish and lobster in it. Thinking he had dropped it by accident, I swam over and grabbed the bag and began ascending with it above my head so that it actually came out of the water first.

As soon as I cleared the water with my head I spat out my regulator and said, "You dropped the bag." He just stared at me with this dumb-founded look and I heard a voice behind me say: "Give me that bag." I turned around and looked over my shoulder and saw two men in a boat with "Marine Patrol" on its hull. As I have said before I may not be the brightest star in the heavens, but I was bright enough to know that they must have asked my buddy for the bag, too, which was why he dropped it.

Well, I thought, if they wanted this bag so badly then I should just drop it, too. So I said "what bag?" and dropped it, thinking they would never be able to retrieve it from the bottom of the ocean. Boy was I wrong. Really wrong. As a matter of fact, I was at the wrong place at the wrong time with the wrong people. It just so happened that one of the men in the boat was a seasoned marine patrol office and the other was a new recruit in training. The old veteran was bound and determined to show his young partner how it was done. He ordered the young man to dive down and confiscate the bag of precious evidence. After several attempts he finally got the bag and my buddy and I got placed into the boat and handcuffed. The charge? Getting lobster out of season.

That had never crossed my mind. It was kind of like paying taxes that first year. At first I thought we were being busted for diving without a dive flag or something. I had no earthly idea that we were breaking the law and surely didn't think we could go to jail for such a thing ... but we did. Seems it was very important to train the young officer properly, especially when it was at the expense of two guys having fun on vacation unaware that they were breaking the law. As we pulled off in the boat we could see our wives standing on the shore, so we just waved and smiled as if we had just paid for a joy ride around the harbor with Florida's finest.

We ended up in jail where they booked us for interfering with Marine Patrol because both of us had dropped the bag of treasure, for diving without a dive flag, and for getting lobster out of season. There I sat in jail just like old times, only now, as a minister and chaplain, I was asking myself how it had happened. Our wives soon bonded us out and we went and had a very solemn dinner and went to bed. The next morning I headed down to city hall to argue the charges. When I got there, however, I learned that they had already dropped all the charges except for getting lobster out of season, for which they fined me $1,000. It was the most expensive seafood I ever bought, and I didn't even get to eat it. My guess was that the veteran Marine Patrol officer had a great meal that night at our expense.

When I look back on that day I often ask myself what possessed me to drop that bag. Most people would not have. They would have handed it over to the officers. For me, however, it came so natural to think "no evidence, no charge." I was very disappointed in myself for not passing that test. Even though I felt very strongly that they were making examples of us (especially since two of the three charges were dismissed the following morning) and that the punishment ($1,000) didn't fit the crime. Regardless, I should have responded differently. Even though I had no malicious intent I was obviously in the wrong and I knew it.

This episode turned out to be a great opportunity for me to see just how much further I needed to go in my spiritual walk. There is a point we reach in our walk with God when we won't respond that way, but I had not gotten there yet. And to be honest I'm not completely there now, either. I still struggle with abuses of power, the "system," Rome, and the ways of the world, but as a Christian I must submit myself to the governing authorities and let Christ be my Advocate. God gave me a great verse of scripture—Mark 15:3-5—a long time ago that I have had to use over and over. This verse tells how Jesus was standing in front of Pontus Pilate after His arrest:

"And the chief priests accused Him of many things, but He answered nothing. Then Pilate asked Him again, saying, 'Do You answer nothing? See how many things they testify against You!' But Jesus still answered nothing, so that Pilate marveled."

You see, we can reach a place in our relationship with God that empowers us even when we are being falsely accused, misjudged, or mistreated to just keep our mouth shut and answer nothing. The Bible says that Pilate marveled at this. In other words he was standing there in awe that this Man wasn't even going to defend His actions. *How could someone not try to plead for his very own life?* Pilate must have been thinking: "Man, if I were you I'd be singing like a canary to escape that cross you're about to hang on and yet you say nothing."

But Jesus wasn't thinking that. His eyes were on His Father. He knew where He would be within the next 24 hours. His body was here, but His heart and His eyes were fixed on home. He was probably thinking something like this: "I'm not going to keep defending Myself. It would do no good anyway. I'm putting this in my Father's hands and letting Him be My Advocate. You'll see the truth one day when I'm not all shackled up, beaten and bruised, and looking like I am the problem instead of the answer. One day I'll be restored to my rightful place, and you will understand then that things were really not the way they seemed."

Spiritual Growth One Trial at a Time

That's the mindset that we should all aspire to. Although I am trying so desperately to get there myself I often find that I fall short. And yet as each new trial approaches, I find that I have grown a little from the last one. It is just like lifting weights. As I said earlier, during my last year or so in prison I began to really hit the weights pretty hard. I noticed that if I just added a little extra weight each time I worked out I grew stronger. I went from benching 135 pounds to benching 405 pounds, and the way

I did it was by adding five pounds at a time—two-and-a-half pounds to each end of the bar—until I got there. A muscle will grow only through pain and resistance. Every time we are confronted with a new trial we should look at it as another five pounds added to the bar of life. The Apostle James tells us, "My brethren, count it all joy when you fall into various trials, knowing that the testing of your faith produces patience. But let patience have *its* perfect work, that you may be perfect and complete, lacking nothing" (James 1:2-4).

Perfect and complete, lacking nothing. Perfect and complete, lacking nothing. The Lord helps us attain that perfect completeness by allowing us to face the trials of life. He will continue to add a little weight each time as we mature as believers. He is treating us as sons and daughters, and like any other loving father He wants us to be at our best. It is up to us to embrace the trials of life and allow them to make us better individuals—to make us more like Jesus Christ, the Author and Perfecter of our faith. The Bible says that Jesus Himself learned obedience through the things that He suffered. How much more then should we expect to have to suffer in order to attain that complete obedience? *Perfect and complete, lacking nothing.*

Praise Him that He loves us just as we are yet far too much to leave us in our original state. Instead, He propels us forward towards that perfected state. Lacking nothing sounds great to me.

CHAPTER 8

FALLING FORWARD

THE MASONRY BUSINESS was doing so well that I began to buy and develop real estate. I bought duplexes, apartments, houses, office buildings, and commercial property. I also began to invest in various business ventures. A friend and I partnered to open a World's Gym in Peachtree City, Georgia, and over the years expanded to three locations. Two other investments went south and cost me quite a bit of money. I wish I could say that I had a perfect record in business, but I can't. It is just like life: You win some and you lose some. The object is to not get too discouraged when you lose. The old saying has it that "winners never quit and quitters never win." They say that if you find a person who will not quit then you have found a winner. Abraham Lincoln was such a man. I have a wall-hanging in my office that inspires me every time I read it.

Abraham Lincoln on Success and Failure
"My great concern is not whether you have failed, but whether you are content with your failure."
– Abraham Lincoln"

Failure can either make us or break us. Those broken by failure are haunted by unpleasant memories that lurk like dark shadows in front, behind, beside, beneath, and above. Those memories are a cage that traps the mind, preventing it from entertaining possibilities of freedom and success. They convince us that they cannot do it and thus they will not even try.

Those whom failure could not break become "made men." Failure to them is not a ghost that inspires fear but a friend who taught them well. They see failure as a stepping stone to wisdom. These men and women are convinced that true failure only happens when one gives up.

History has been kind to President Abraham Lincoln. He is considered by many to be the greatest president in American history. It is a good thing that history also recorded his failures that show both his frail humanity and his determined attitude of never giving up.

President Lincoln's failures could not stop him. He kept moving forward. The following is a short list of his ups and downs and ups:

*1831 – Failed in business

1832 – Defeated for legislature

1833 – Failed in business again

1834 – Elected to legislature

1835 – Sweetheart died

1836 – Had a nervous breakdown

1838 – Defeated for speaker

1840 – Defeated for elector

1843 – Defeated for Congress

1846 – Elected for Congress

1848 – Defeated for Congress

1855 – Defeated for Senate

1856 – Defeated for Vice President

1858 – Defeated for Senate

1860 – ELECTED PRESIDENT

Lincoln was defeated many more times than he won, but that did not mean he was a failure. Remember: *Failures are only permanent if we stop trying and the only real failure is the failure not to move on.*

Yes, life is like that. It is going to throw you curve balls, and if you do not learn how to hit them you will find yourself beat down and beat on.

I think the number one reason that so many of the men in our ministry relapse on drugs and alcohol is that they get tired of fighting the temptation and just throw in the towel. Sometimes you just get tired of fighting.

I wish I could tell you that I never failed again, but I can't. In fact, I stumbled and fell during these days of prosperity. I can honestly say that I didn't set out intentionally to do it. I made the mistake one more time of thinking that I could drink alcohol.

I have been something of a health nut since I started working out in prison. I read *Muscle & Fitness* magazine, watch my diet, and work out six days a week. I really got too involved and too consumed with weight training. It was out of balance. It is kind of like that Harley Davidson emblem that says "live to ride and ride to live." I have a Harley but I sure don't live to ride it or need to ride it to live. Nor do I need to lift weights and worry about the size and density of every muscle group of my body. But it all stems from that old belief that *if a little is good then a lot will be great.* Take it from me, that is not always so.

Here's how it happened. I ended up drinking a glass of wine because I had read in umpteen different magazines that it was good for a man's heart and would prolong his life. So, since I didn't like the taste of red wine I figured I was safe and that I would simply incorporate one glass a day into my diet. Wrong move. I did great for a while until I acquired a taste for the wine and really began enjoying it. Well, it wasn't long before one glass became two and before I knew it I was having a "few." Then, just like in the old days, one night I drank too much, called an old buddy, did some cocaine, and failed miserably one last time.

The next day I called a dear friend and spiritual mentor and told him what had happened. He jumped in his car and drove from the other side of Atlanta to my house and prayed with me. That was the last time I ever drank or did drugs. Lesson learned! I have never done that again nor will I. I knew once and for all that alcohol would never again grace my lips. I tell my guys all the time: You are only one drink away from failure. Stay away at all cost.

Not long thereafter the guy who brought the cocaine over that night committed suicide—just one more casualty in the war on drugs. He was a Christian living in a backslidden state and just couldn't get free.

A Long-Lost Son Comes Home

One day I got a call from my first wife, Laurie, whom I had not spoken to since she went back to Tacoma, Washington, some 12 years earlier. She told me that our son, whom I had never seen nor talked to, was having problems and asked me if I could help. The last I had heard was that she had remarried, had more children, and was very involved in church. I had always assumed that our son Josh was in good hands in a well-balanced home and that life was good. I had no idea that he was in such a bad state of mind and was having major issues. After Laurie left me I began my slow but steady decline, and she and I both felt it was best to cut ties and just let her and her new husband raise Josh as if I didn't exist. We were 3,000 miles apart and I could not afford to fly back and forth to build a relationship, especially given the way I was living, and I was back in prison before long anyway.

So this surprise call came as a real shocker. It was really strange to go from the one whom nobody trusted or believed in to the one people were beginning to reach out to for help. It felt good being the solution rather than the problem. I told Laurie that I would call her back after discussing the situation with my wife. In talking with Lindsey we felt that nobody was more suited to help Josh than I because I had been there and done that. So I called Laurie and told her that we would love to have him come and live with us, and then I sent her a plane ticket for him. I will never forget the day he arrived. My wife, my dad, my mom, my grandmother, and a few others all went to the airport to greet him.

We were all excited and when the plane landed we stood at the door waiting eagerly to see Josh as he walked off the plane. A few passengers began trickling out when this fellow who looked like a businessman came out and said, "Any of you guys waiting on Josh?" We all replied in a happy unified voice: "Yes." At that the guy said, "Well, you're in for a hell of a treat." There was no smile on his face. Needless to say we all felt as though we had been hit in the stomach. The man looked like he had just made parole himself by getting off that plane. A few minutes later Josh walked out and we were all shocked. He was dressed in all black and had a ghetto blaster (radio) on his shoulder and was listening to rap music. I immediately began connecting the dots.

Dot one: Why would a mother send her son 3,000 miles away?

Dot two: Why would that businessman say what he had just said?

Dot three: Josh had my genes in him.

Dot four: He was dressed in all black and was listening to rap music.

Dot five: My wife Lindsey was going to kill me.

I wish I could report that we were able to help Josh get his life together, but we were not. We tried everything we knew—from church, to affection, to tough love, to time-outs, to gifts, to ... everything. Nothing worked with Josh. He was kicked out of school shortly thereafter, put on probation, sentenced to juevenile, and then ended up in the same YDC that I was in for five years. He got out when he was 18, went right back to making wrong choices, and was killed by the Fulton County Swat Team in a drug raid when he was 24 years old. Josh had gotten involved with the Russian Mafia and got mixed up with the wrong people. I will never forget the night they called me and informed me of his death. Nothing can prepare you for a call like that. It will be with me for the rest of my life. Josh is buried on our property near a chapel that I built when I first bought the place. His headstone has the scripture Genesis 50:20 on it: "What the enemy means for harm God means for good that many people's lives will be saved."

I sometimes stand new men in our ministry in front of his tombstone and allow them to look at his grave and at the chapel at the same time. I remind them that they have a choice to make. They can either choose life or they can choose death. The choice is theirs. My hope is that looking at Josh's grave will sober them so that God can use Josh's death to help the next man make a better choice. It is all about falling—or as some have put it: *failing*—forward and getting mileage out of the mess. We must strive to capitalize on every move the enemy makes so that God can take what the enemy means for harm and use it for good. I believe the best for Josh. I had seen him at the altar of the church on occasion when he first came to live with us weeping, confessing his sins, and asking God to come into his heart. I also led him to the water a multitude of times, and I am praying that he will be in heaven and that his conversion was real.

This type of thing can really make a person ponder. *What part did I have to play in this? Would Josh be alive today had I been there as a father?* I don't know. I know there are a lot of single moms and a lot of children with step-moms and dads who turn out great. Although his life ended in a very unlikely manner, I still find myself asking how his life might have been different if I had made different choices. King David also had to wrestle with such thoughts. He, too, lost his son Absalom who, like Josh, chose the wrong way. Absalom refused to listen to his father's counsel and instead rebelled against authority. In the end Joab, David's own general, killed Absalom in order to protect David's life.

The Bible says that when David received the news that his son was dead, his grief lead him to tear his clothes and cry out that he wished he himself had died in his son's place. He then ordered that a great heap of stones be erected where Absalom had fallen as a memorial to his name. God has given us the story of King David and many others in the Bible so that we can find hope when things look hopeless. So many characters in the Bible were just like you and me. They suffered the same losses and enjoyed the same victories. They had to process the same feelings and deal with the same kind of issues as we do.

That is why the Word of God is so important, especially in times of crisis. It brings us sorely needed comfort as we learn that we are not alone in our struggles, and it helps keep us moving forward as we see that there is life after failure and light at the end of our tunnel. Jesus Christ is the Light of the world, and the Bible is our God-given instruction manual for our lives. We need light to see our way through this dark world, and if we will simply open up the instruction manual then the

Light will surely illuminate its precious contents and enable us to see clearly how to travel on this sometimes wearying journey. Another thing about light is that it gives off heat. Light is always warm and we will always feel the warmth of the scriptures as we embrace them and make them our own. Praise Him for always being there to comfort us in our time of need.

A Bittersweet Turn: A Reminder of God's Unfailing Love

I am not sure how it unfolded in Heaven, but the very same day my son Josh died my granddaughter Selah was born. My daughter Hollie, who was still struggling at that time, gave birth to Selah on October 9. Lindsey and I actually adopted Selah and her two brothers, Israel and Joshua. They have been with us since Selah was born and the boys were two and five. Selah's being born on the same day that we lost Josh made for a very bittersweet day. That was no coincidence, however. I know that in His sovereignty the Lord did a very special thing that day. Every year

Riding with Selah

on the anniversary of Josh's death we are able to look at a beautiful little girl and be reminded of God's great love for us. I think I know how King David must have felt when he looked at young Solomon after Absalom's death.

The name "Selah" means "to ponder and meditate on." When David wrote the Psalms he would write the word "selah" out beside certain psalms. What he was saying to those who would read it in the future (as well as for himself right then) was: Stop for a moment and meditate on this verse a little longer. He was saying that this scripture held a special place in his heart above the rest and was thus worthy of more attention. It was the same with that special day—the day of Selah's birth. The Lord did something very wonderful when He brought Selah into the world, and every October 9 we are reminded once again that His love never fails and that we are all special in His sight.

Lindsey and I consider ourselves blessed to be allowed to help the Lord raise four wonderful children. They are all very precious souls. So far God has enabled us to keep them in Christian schools, involved in a great church, playing sports, and involved in many other positive things. We are really trying hard to sow into their lives all the things that were not sown into ours and to teach them all the lessons that we learned the hard way. Our hope and prayer is that we can help pave a much smoother road for them to walk on.

CHAPTER 9

A DIVINE APPOINTMENT: A BETTER WAY MINISTRIES

A FEW MONTHS BEFORE that bittersweet day, October 9, I went out looking for some land to buy to develop for a subdivision when I stumbled across a piece of property in Coweta County. We had mailed letters to residents in a particular area asking if they were interested in selling their property, and out of all of the letters we sent we received only one response. It came from a little old lady named Miss Christopher who owned about 50 acres on Christopher Road. It seemed just like the Lord to send us land on a road that had His name in it— *Christ.*

I will never forget the day that I pulled onto the property for the first time. I was on the phone talking with my wife, and as I pulled into the driveway I looked out the window at all of the old barns dating back to the early 1900s, giant old oak trees, beautiful land, and thought to myself: "There is no way I could ruin the beauty of this place by developing it." I also mentioned this to Lindsey on the phone.

As I parked my truck I spotted Miss Christopher sitting in a swing on the front porch of the old farm house. I hung up with my wife and got out and introduced myself. Miss Christopher told me that she had not been thinking about selling the property, but some things had changed recently that made her think that maybe it was time. She went on to tell me the story of the Christophers and how she became one. She was not a Christopher by birth but had married into the family. Her husband had recently passed away leaving her with this 50-acre piece of land and the original farm house that all of the Christophers had been born and raised in since the early 1900s. She pointed to a 60-acre plot to her left and said, "He's a Christopher"; she pointed to a 60-acre plot to her right and said, "They are Christophers"; and then she pointed across the street at a 200-acre plot and said, "They are Christophers as well."

As I have said before I might be one sandwich shy of a picnic, but I have enough in the basket to figure out some things. One thing was for sure: It made absolutely no sense for all these Christophers to allow her to sell the old home place that they had all been raised in. Why would they not buy it and keep it in the family? I mean they even owned the road, didn't they? You know, *Christopher* Road. Why would they not want to preserve the oldest landmark? When I asked her about it, she responded that she would definitely have to ask them if they wanted to purchase it first before she could commit to me. So we negotiated a price, and she said she would get back with me soon and let me know the verdict.

Well I never thought we would get the land. It just didn't add up. I knew one of them would decide to keep it or they would come together and purchase it as a family. But it didn't happen. Before long Miss Christopher called and told me that although all the Christopher kin wanted the land they simply didn't have the money to buy it. She accepted my offer and asked me when I could close. I told her it would be within a few weeks. I wanted to move pretty fast in case her "kin" found one of those Mason jars the late Mr. Christopher hid out in the field and suddenly had the funds to buy it themselves. So I secured a loan rather quickly and bought it within the month.

When I got it, however, I had no idea what I was going to do with it. All I knew was that God had somehow put me right in the middle of a divine appointment and that He had confirmed it through different

Chapel on property

fleeces I had put out. When we closed on the property I had great peace in my spirit and was certain that this transaction was much more than just a piece of land even though I couldn't yet see the whole picture yet. So for the next few months I went out there almost daily to walk, pray, and seek God for His guidance. Each time I went I seemed to find myself in the same place. It was on a small knoll right above a little pond directly in the middle of the property. Before long, I found myself building a small chapel on the site out of cedar, cypress, and stones, which were the building materials King Solomon used to build the temple in the Bible.

I put in some stained glass, ran power to it, and furnished it with some cedar benches and two rocking chairs made by the Amish. It became a quiet place of solitude and prayer. I had many precious encounters with the Lord there and received many a word from Him for the future of the ministry that was about to come. I still use it today as a place to pray and seek His guidance and counsel. I also use it for small weddings and memorials to marry and bury people. It has become a landmark on the property and just as the Lord told Solomon that His spirit would reside in the temple, His spirit resides in that little chapel. It is a very special place.

Start a Ministry Here...

Looking back I must say that it was there that the Lord put it on my heart to start a ministry for men like I used to be—men who couldn't seem to break free from addiction to drugs or alcohol; men who wanted to "get it right" but just couldn't; men who, if given a good place to become spiritually enriched, just might be able to get clean and stabilize once and for all. So I then began to reach out to a Teen Challenge ministry on the other side of Atlanta. They helped me get started by sending me five men and a great leader named Brother Phillip. They also introduced me to a man named Tony Ingram who lived close to me and wanted to start a ministry as well. Tony eventually became my director as well as a dear friend. And so it was. We started *A Better Way Ministries* with an old farm house, 50 acres of land, a small chapel, five students, Brother Phillip, Brother Tony, me, and a word from God. And that was all it took.

Things began growing faster than I could ever have imagined. It was as if somebody had doused us with Miracle Grow. Square Foot Ministries from Fayetteville, Georgia, came out and did what they call "a blitz build" on the old farm house. It was like the TV show "Extreme Makeover – Home Edition." With the help of a few local churches in just four weeks they turned an old 1,200 square foot farmhouse into a 3,000 square foot nicely renovated home. Men soon began showing up on our doorstep telling us that they had heard about us from so and so. Before long it was very obvious that the Lord's thumbprint was on this ministry and that He wanted to do a great work here.

Most visions from God require us to practice our faith. I soon discovered that continuing to support this endeavor was going to take more money than I had thought. Nine out of 10 of the men who were coming to us showed up penniless. They had burned all their bridges, damaged all their relationships, and borrowed their last dime. Usually by the time they got to us no one was there to help support them during their stay. One thing that's sure about men who get off drugs and clean up their act up is that they begin to eat, and eat, and eat. I mean to say they eat a lot. After missing all those meals while they were out there in the world living on a liquid and powder diet they were very hungry and had a lot of missed meals to make up for. And guess what? It cost money to feed, house, and equip hungry men.

We now have about 50 men in our ministry, and if you can imagine what a herd of locusts will do to a field of grain, you will get a pretty good idea of what we look like when we sit down to eat. We can literally pray Joel 2:25 in two ways now: The way my grandmother prayed it for me and "Lord, please restore what these locusts just ate away because we are now out of food." In the beginning I thought I would be able to get local churches, friends, and other ministries to sustain the ministry financially, but that didn't happen. I learned very quickly that just because something is dear to your heart does not mean that you can expect it to be dear to anyone else's. We all have different callings to different types of

ABW men at Christmas church service

ABW men performing a Fishing for Men drama at local parade

ministry and we cannot expect everyone to feel the same way that we do about what God has called us to.

Another thing I learned is that it is a lot harder to raise financial support for men than it is to raise it for women's or children's ministry. Most people think that men should go out and work to support themselves, and they are right. I believe the same thing. I have always had a strong work ethic and don't believe in taking hand-outs. Our ministry motto is "Help me help you." We believe in doing something to earn what is given. I have always been the type of guy who will help those who help themselves. Otherwise I feel as though I am just wasting my resources and time and continuing to enable them. The only problem with this approach in this type of support ministry is that the more we work the students, the less time we have to disciple them. It is a catch-22 sometimes. We must work to pay the bills, but at the same time we must disciple the men because *that* is why we are here. More work equals less discipleship.

One thing that I say over and over to myself and the leadership is "this is a ministry first, not a business." I had plenty of businesses and surely didn't want to start another one, especially with 50 broken men who couldn't manage themselves much less run a company. It can be very challenging to stay balanced in this type of environment. We are constantly being stretched to meet the bills and keep everything afloat. Even after seven years we are still check-to-check. I am thankful that I have never needed to draw a salary from this ministry to sustain my family because if I did I don't know how we would have made it..

The reason that so many ministries start and then fizzle out is that they can't raise enough support to keep them afloat especially if the director / founder needs to be paid to support his own livelihood. Over the last seven years we have been truly blessed in being able to start a multitude of cottage industries to help support ourselves. We now have a moving company with 14 trucks, a sign shop, a café, a thrift store, a wood shop, an automotive repair shop, a lawn care business, a local magazine, and one or two other small enterprises. God has enabled us to be self sustaining, and we have never had to turn a man away. Praise Him for His faithfulness!

An Audible Word from the Lord: "Cast Out into the Deep..."

One morning in the early stages of the ministry I was sitting on my couch before dawn doing my morning devotions when I heard an audible voice behind me. It was so audible that I turned my head around and looked over my shoulder. Since I was the only person up at that hour I knew that it must be the voice of the Holy Spirit. All He said was "Luke 5:4." That's it. No "John," no nothing. Just "Luke 5:4." My Bible was open on my lap so I quickly turned to Luke 5:4 to see what it said. When I landed on it I couldn't really understand its significance. All it said was "cast out into the deep and let down your nets for a catch." *Go fishing? What are you saying, Lord?*

I spent the next year or so marinating in that verse of scripture and allowing the Lord to show me what He meant by it. Jesus was telling Peter at that time to go out further into the Sea of Galilee and drop his net down. Peter had been fishing all night and obviously thought Jesus didn't know what He was talking about because Peter told Him: "I have been fishing these waters all night and have caught nothing, however at your word I will do as you say." Well when they got out into the deeper water and let down their net they caught so many fish that the net began to break and they needed help from other boats to get the fish to land. When he saw this miraculous event Peter fell to his knees and told the Lord, "Away from me for I am a sinful man." Jesus then said, "Peter, from now on you will catch souls, not fish."

So what the Lord told me that morning was this: "John, if you will obey Me and trust Me enough to go deeper, then I will send so many men and so much provision that your net will not be able to contain it. You are no longer to put your work first because your priority from now on must be souls." After I got saved in prison I began noticing such passages of scripture that pointed me to this very conclusion. I had been side-stepping it for a long time. Some of those scriptures were:

Luke 12:48: "For everyone who is given much, much is now required."

Mathew 25:14-30: The Parable of the Talents that tells us we are required to do something with what God gives us and not just bury it in the sand.

Luke 13:8: The owner of the vineyard tells the gardener to cut down the tree because it produces no fruit, and the gardener begs him for one more year so that he can fertilize it, water it, prune it, etc., in hopes that he can get the tree to produce what it should be producing.

Many more passages of scripture compel us to do something for the Kingdom. You see, I always felt that more was required of me given the grace that God had bestowed on me and the gift He had given me by allowing me to live through all that I had lived through, while so many around me had died. I liken it to Jesus' encounter with Peter on the beach (John 21) in which Christ asked him three times, "Peter, do you love me?" Why would Jesus ask Peter that question three times and then respond with, "Then feed my sheep"? This is the only passage in scripture in which Jesus asks the same question three times. Most people think it was just to restore Peter after his denial of Him, but that is not so.

The thing that most don't see—and I wouldn't have seen either had the Lord not provoked me to study the life of Peter—is that the first time He asked Peter the question "Do you love Me," He added "more than these." He said: "Do you love Me more than these?" The context was that Peter had just dragged another record-breaking catch of fish to the shore. They were lying right beside them as Jesus began His second commission of Peter (the first was when He first called Peter who was fishing on the Sea of Galilee and he bade Peter to follow Him so that He could make him a fisher of men; Matthew 4:18-19). Peter had just walked by the other disciples, as though he was going back to life as usual after Jesus was crucified, and they asked him, "Peter, where are you going?" He told them, "I am going fishing," and they said, "We are going with you." They then proceeded to fall back to the *same old same old* of being led by Peter, just as they had been when Jesus first called them. They were fishing for the sake of fishing until Jesus showed up on the beach and got them back on track.

On a trip to Jerusalem a while back I visited the Sea of Galilee and saw a bronze memorial emblazoned with the words: "Place of Peter's second commissioning." You see this was the second time Christ had to literally shame Peter into action. On His first encounter He had plainly told Peter that he was to fish for souls from that day forward and not just fish for

Peter's second commissioning near the Sea of Galilee

fish. And now He was telling him again, "Peter, if you love me then show it. Why did you lead these others back to fishing for fish and not fishing for souls? Have you forgotten who you are so soon? Don't you remember something being said about My church being built on you? Remember that, Peter? So, then, how is that going to happen out there in that boat? You say that you love Me more than all these fish you just dragged onto shore, or these other disciples that are sitting here around you, but you are not showing it by what you are doing with your life. I've been gone less than a month, and you're right back to life as usual. Your priorities have shifted so quickly."

Does anybody know what I'm talking about here? That was how it was for me as well. I was a slow responder. It took a "Do you love Me?" three times experience before I got it as well. Only in my case it was maybe *300* times. The Bible says that faith without works is dead. It is one thing to say you love someone and quite another to show it. In 2 Peter 1:1 Peter referred to himself as a "bondservant of Jesus Christ." A bondservant in Jesus' day was a servant who served *by choice*. This type of servant didn't start out that way, though. They were usually bought from another owner at a price; they were sold into slavery, so to speak. Once purchased they served under obligation for a specified number of years, usually seven, at which time they were allowed to go free. If they so chose, however, they could go to their owner and say something like this, "I really love it here. Your family has become like my family. I love your children. You have been good to me. Your land is like my land. Can I please stay here with you and your family because I would like to serve you out of my heart instead of out of obligation?"

If the master agreed to let the servant stay, he would lead the servant to the front door of his house, place his earlobe on the doorpost, and then hammer a small shank into his ear to signify that the servant was no longer just a servant but a *bond*servant who served by choice rather than obligation. I, like Peter and many others, did not begin serving the Lord just because we loved Him or because we knew that it was the right thing to do. We may have started out serving him due to tragedy, pain, failure, etc. After being in His family of believers, however, and serving in His house and getting to know Him intimately, we came to a point in our walk that there was no other place on earth we would rather be than yoked to Him. We thus no longer serve Him out of obligation but out of love and devotion.

I have the word "Bondservant" tattooed across the top of my back as a constant reminder of what I am and what I have committed to be. I now serve by choice. There is no other place I would rather be.

CHAPTER 10

TWO ASTONISHING MILESTONES

Pardon Me, Pastor...

Somewhere along this road of sanctification two milestones occurred in my life. The first occurred one day as I was sitting in my office. One of the girls who worked for me at the time walked up to my desk and said, "John, have you ever thought about asking for a pardon from the Department of Corrections for your crimes? You are a Chaplain for them, you do so much good for people, and it's been so long now that I bet they would give you one. What do you think?"

I just looked at her thinking how sweet she was and how much I appreciated her kind words and heartfelt emotion, but I also sat there thinking how naïve and gullible she was as well. Then I responded with something like, "Sweetheart, are you OK? Did you forget to take your meds again this morning? It'll be all right, just sit down a moment until it passes."

She said, "I'm serious, John. I believe they should give you a pardon."

I shrugged. "I would come closer to hitting the lottery tonight than getting a pardon for the things I have done. Have you ever seen my record? They don't just hand out pardons to repeat offenders. I appreciate your heart in this, but to answer your question: No, I haven't thought about it and I won't. It would be a complete waste of time."

She then told me that, if I was OK with it, she would like to check into it. To pacify her I told her to go ahead but not to waste much time on it because it was not going to happen. She agreed and walked off smiling.

Well I had kind of forgotten all about it until one day, many months later, I got home from work and checked the mail as was my habit after a long day at work. To my surprise I found a letter from the Department of Corrections addressed to me. I will never forget opening it and reading it right there beside the mailbox. In the past anything that was sent to me with the words "Department of Corrections" on it usually caused my heart to skip a beat. I was afraid they might want to "correct" me some more....

But this time it was far from being anything negative. It was something that any man who had ever been to prison would love to see and something that very few have the honor of receiving. Well, remember how I told the sweet little gullible girl that a pardon was never going to happen? Well, guess what? *It did.* The letter was a pardon with a gold seal on it officially pardoning me of all my past crimes. The dear girl had drawn up a petition and gone around soliciting letters from a multitude of people, including my pastor, the chief of police, lawyers, judges, and others. She then began building her case and went at it with a vengeance to show that I was no longer the same guy I used to be and that I truly had reformed.

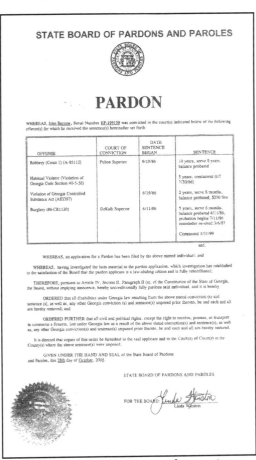

Pardon from the Department of Corrections

Talk about being blown away. *I. Was. Blown. Away.* I had been so sure that a pardon was impossible, that it simply couldn't be done. But all it took was someone who believed in me enough to really go after it and prove to the state that I was a new man. I will always be grateful for what she did for me.

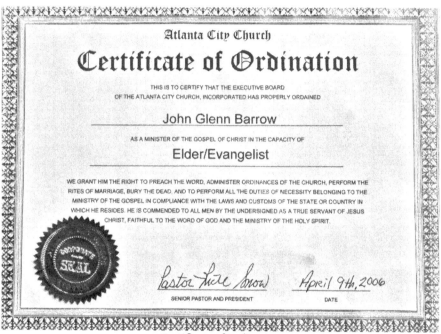

Certificate of Ordination

Another honor bestowed upon me came when I was chosen to be a fellow pastor and elder at my church. I had been attending Atlanta City Church, now known as New City Church, for some time when the pastor asked me if I would be interested in the position. After a very brief period of thinking and praying over it, I said "yes." I sensed deep in my heart that as the days ahead unfolded I would become more and more involved with ministry in one way or another, though I just didn't know how and where. Being chosen at that time to help shepherd God's flock was definitely in line with that goal. Shortly thereafter I was ordained by the church and placed in that position. That was some 10 years ago and

I still serve there today. Our membership has grown to around 1,500 on two campuses, one in Fairburn and another in Peachtree City, Georgia. God has been so good to us! New City is a great church with a great group of passionate believers. It is truly an honor to help God and other great men and women build His house. It is not every day that a person is blessed to go from the prison to the pulpit as well as be pardoned both by God and by man.

For this I will be eternally grateful.

A Better Way Ministries: A Thorn in the Ministry

Starting the ministry on Christopher Road did not come without challenges. One of the questions I asked Miss Christopher when I bought the land from her was whether her family members were Christians. She assured me they were. I figured with a name like *Christ*opher they had to be, right? Well, no. One thing I learned early on in my Christian walk is that people can have very different definitions of what it means to be a Christian. Just as "beauty" is in the eye of the beholder so it seems that being a "Christian" is in the mind of many "so-called" believers. The word Christian means Christ-like. Trust me, you are going to meet *many* who profess Christ and don't act Christ-like.

From day one I was a little concerned about being sandwiched in the middle of a bunch of Christophers—living in their old home place, walking on their old land, and fishing in their old pond. I wondered how they were going to adjust to this new way of life with a "stranger" on their old homestead. Much to my surprise, all but one of them handled it well. One of them does surveying work for us, another does grading for us, and another does our seed and straw. One, however, has been a burr under our saddle and a real pain in the old butt. The rest of the family are quick to point out that he is their cousin and does not represent their views. Looking back now I picture old Miss Christopher begging him to be sweet until the closing was over. She may have even paid him to do so because he hasn't been sweet ever since. Even though we paid half a million dollars for our land he still thinks it is his.

One day soon after we bought the property I took my son Noah, a gallon of oil, some stones, and a shofar (ram's horn) and went to pray over the property. We had planned to go to all four corners, make some little landmarks out of stones, pour oil on them, then blow the shofar in every direction—north, south, east, and west. I know, I know, it's weird, right? (I have always been a little "touched" as some might say anyway, but to me and my way of thinking this was important.) Well we made it through three of the four corners and came to the last one. As we began to build the small stack of stones Mr. Christoper drove up on his four-wheeler and just sat there about 15 feet away, saying nothing, and watched us as we did our little ritual. When I got to the part where I was to blow the shofar I knew he was going to think I was an idiot, which would confirm once and for all that he was right in his assessment.

Although the ritual may sound a little crazy to some, for me it was a spiritual way of praying a blessing and protection over the land. The shofar is a ram's horn that the Israelites would blow on two occasions—one was after a victorious battle to declare victory and the second was to ward off any evil spirits that may be present. Oddly enough, at that moment I felt the second reason was very applicable because there was definitely an evil spirit very close to Noah and me. I also knew that I had come too far to stop and was not going to be deterred by one contrary vote.

So I grabbed my shofar and began to blow it towards all four directions. When I was done I just looked at him to see his response and sure enough he had one. He just looked down at us like we were a freak show exhibit at the county fair and said, "Y'all sho' are emotional folks at y'all's church, ain't ya? We don't get into all that emotion out here." He then just grunted and rode off the way he rode in except now he no doubt was enjoying the pleasure of belittling me in front of my son and making fun of the way I was teaching Noah to honor God.

Looking back, things began to change when he heard the words "drug addicts and alcoholics" and saw men who weren't all white folk start showing up on "his" property. It was then that he began trying his best to make life unbearable for us. He started riling up his family, other neighbors, and whomever he could find to start a petition to run us out of the neighborhood, so to speak. Before long we began seeing people riding by taking pictures of the men in hopes of showing that we had too many men living in our home. He and his group of supporters hired a lawyer and pursued legal action aimed at having the county shut us down. This man did just about everything he could do to hurt us. But it all came to nothing. Well, all except for one thing....

One day I got a visit from a county code enforcement officer, who I later found out was a friend of his. (I would have guessed he didn't have any.) The officer handed me four citations and informed me that he would see me in court. The citations were for building a chapel without a permit, building a barn without a permit, building a barn too close to the property line, and letting our horses roam beyond the fence. When I entered the courtroom, Mr. Christopher was sitting on the back row looking like he just couldn't wait for the show to begin. You know how snitches think. They have this weird thing going on between those two ears hanging on the left and right sides of their head. I guess he was hoping the judge would sentence me to life in prison for my atrocious crimes.

And to be honest, I was a little concerned myself. I held a state-issued builder's license and knew that I wasn't supposed to build anything without a permit—although I can honestly say that when I was building the little chapel my mind never once thought about a permit. I mean, if you can't build a place to pray on 52 acres without notifying the governing authorities, then what can you do? I had just come from a subdivision with one-acre lots and felt as though I was living on a ranch in Montana.

The judge read off each charge and asked me how I wished to plead. I responded: guilty, guilty, guilty, and guilty. (I had a lot of practice at this.) He then asked me if I wished to say anything about this and I said, "Yes, I would." I told him: "Your honor, this isn't about a chapel, a barn, or a horse, but about a man who doesn't want me living on *his* property trying to help men with drug and alcohol problems."

The judge then looked at the old code enforcement officer and asked if that were true. The officer denied it, of course, and said that I was just a rebel who didn't want to abide by the law. (He had no earthly idea what I looked like as a rebel.) So the judge put his little bi-focals on his nose and studied all the pictures of my chapel and barn that they had entered as evidence. After a moment or two he looked over the tops of his glasses and said, "Mr. Barrow, did you build this chapel?" I said, "Yes, sir, your honor." He looked back down at the pictures and without looking up said, "You think you could build me one of these?" I said, "I sure could, your honor." A huge smile starting to arise down in my belly.

He then looked at me and said, "Mr Barrow, since you pleaded guilty, the minimum I can fine you on these charges is $150 per occurrence, which amounts to $600.00, but I can combine them all into one if you want. Do you think you can afford to pay $150 today?" I said, "I sure can, your honor." (I could see the Lord just a smiling as well.) About this time I heard a little ruffling behind me as my neighbor, the lovely Mr. Christopher, stormed out of the courtroom. The code enforcement officer just stood there looking as though he had been hit square in the head with a frying pan. I paid the $150, thanked my Lord in heaven and the judge on earth, and went home.

I continued trying to be kind to Mr. Christopher as he continued spurning us and trying to make life difficult for us. I got to the point where every time he did something harsh, I would do something nice. Over the course of a year or two I had my secretary send him numerous Honey Baked Hams, flower arrangements, and even homemade cookies. I tried smothering him with kindness even though my flesh wanted to do something else. The Bible tells us that "vengeance is mine, saith the Lord," but I must confess that sometimes I ask God if I can help Him out just a wee bit.

One of those times was the day my wife Lindsey called me at work all upset because the horses had gotten out again and wandered over to Mr.

Christopher's yard. So I told her to take another girl who was at our house and run out and get them quickly before he saw them. But it was too late. By the time they got over there Mr. Christopher had both of the horses in lock-up and refused to let the girls have them. He had tied them up and called his code enforcement buddy. So I left my office hotter than fire over the fact that this had turned into harassment and, well, I had never played well in school being harassed. If you want to hit me, fine, then hit me, but don't keep thumping me on the back of my head every time you pass by.

As it turned out, before I got home it was all over. Mr. Christopher was back in his house, the horses were back in the fence, code enforcement had left, and the girls were shaking it off. Looking back, I should have been praising the Lord because if I had gotten home any sooner I might have landed in big trouble. It is one thing to mess with me, and quite another to mess with my wife and another defenseless young girl. At such times as these, however, the man of God is being made. It is when the heat gets the hottest that the impurities begin to surface. The Bible says that in our anger we must not sin. Of course, this is much easier said than done. And to be honest, I was sinning inside at this point. I really wanted to walk over to his house, drag him out in his backyard, and give his code enforcement buddy a reason for another citation. My anger was burning so hot that I actually had a hard time sleeping that night.

It's Not What Happens, But How We Respond

It is strange how once the ball of injustice is passed to the believer it is no longer about the one who passed it but the believer who receives it. It was no longer about Mr. Christopher's wrong but about how I would process and deal with that wrong. Would I allow *it* to consume me or would I rise above it and let *God* consume me? Would I focus on the infraction or look beyond it? Could I see Mr. Christopher in another light—perhaps as a man who could not see outside his own box, as a man I should pray for because of his tunnel vision and narrow-minded views? Was he just a product of his environment, being raised in a narrow-minded era? Or was I going to respond like most and say, "OK, you hit me so now I'm going to hit you." It is all about the response. The way we respond will always dictate whether or not we will have to take the test over again. The quicker we learn, the quicker we go on to a harder test. Sounds fun, doesn't it? I wish I could say I passed this test with flying colors, but I didn't. Though I didn't do anywhere near as badly as I would have before, I certainly didn't do as well as I could have, either. I am definitely still a WIP—a work in process.

As so often happens the next morning I felt better—not great, but better. So I got up, read the Word, prayed, got dressed, and left for work. I had somewhat of a so-so day and found myself heading home sort of early. I went and sat out on the porch with the guys in the ministry. As we were talking one of the most wonderful experiences of my life happened. We saw this dog come around the side of the house and approach us. One of the guys said, "That's Mr. Christopher's dog." I said, "Are you kidding me?" They all confirmed it. At this point I looked towards the heavens and said, "Thank You, Lord, for sending the deliverer." I quickly grabbed the dog, directed the guys to place him in a transport vehicle, whisked him away to a secure hostage holding location (a friend's house), and prepared for negotiations to begin the very next morning. I figured since he held my horses hostage I could hold his dog hostage. *Right?* My goal was to give him a taste of his own medicine.

I was just going to keep his animal a little longer than he had kept mine, but I wasn't going to call the law. That's one thing I learned in juvenile— that you never bring "the man" into it unless you absolutely have to. The law is the last resort. The code holds that you never snitch on anyone, right? So I figured I'd just handle the situation myself—speaking the language old Mr. Christopher could understand. I told my wife Lindsey that I was going to Wal-Mart to buy some little stick-on letters and make a ransom note that said: "If you ever want to see your dog alive again you must quit bothering the Barrow family and A Better Way Ministries." Maybe even make a reality show out of it.

Well, I didn't. Thanks to my wife, my secretary, and the Holy Spirit, I only kept the pooch 24 hours or so. I had planned to keep him for at least three days, making it spiritual, like Jonah in the belly of the whale, or Jesus in the tomb, something to help me feel better about my vengeance, but the Holy Spirit wouldn't allow it. He began to work on me through the voices of two women who had my ear at all times. I had done so well up to that point and here I was blowing it by messing with the man. I had stooped down to his level by doing this. I can honestly say that I wasn't doing it to hurt him or get back at him but to get him to back off and let us be. I was sick and tired of the harassment and didn't know how to stop it. If not for the facts that I was a Christian, a pastor, and fairly well-known in the community, I would have given him a big dose of his own bitter medicine a long time ago. So in my mind this was really a mild and harmless way of getting his attention.

The very next night I got on my golf cart, put the dog in my lap, and headed over to his house. When he came to the door and saw me standing there with the dog he just started smiling and looking at his dog as if it were a brand-new super-size pack of Red Man chewing tobacco, the stuff that was splattered down both sides of his truck. (I believe his wife chews, also.) But after the momentary euphoria his smile faded into a sinister stare. He looked at me the way the Wicked Witch of the West looked at Dorothy when she first saw her, as if to say "Oh, you think you're so smart don't you?" He said, "That dog ain't never stayed out over night since we had him." And then he just stared at me and asked, "Was he at your house last night?" To which I replied, "No, he wasn't." Which was the truth. He was at my friend's house.

When he launched into some other accusation I just stopped him and said, "Mr. Christopher, remember how in school when we were little if somebody were to start taking someone else's lunch every day that person who had their lunch taken would have to either go hungry or fight back so he could eat, right? You didn't want to fight, but you realized that if you didn't you would never have lunch again. So it was either fight or starve. So even though you had no desire to fight you soon realized that if you didn't you might as well get used to being abused and just start asking the bully what he would like for lunch the next day so that your mom could fix it for him. You know what I mean, Mr. Christopher?"

His stare became a laser beam. I could have sworn I caught a glimpse of that John Deere tractor he rode in dancing in the tiny pupils of his eyes. "You threatening me?" he said, looking like Dirty Harry with his .44 magnum, to which I replied, "No, I'm not threatening you. I'm just telling you a story. I just want to be left alone." At that I turned around, got in my golf cart, and rode off. That was the night things began to die down and we now live in semi-peace although he still won't wave or acknowledge our presence even though we wave and smile when we see him out in the yard. He is just one more person trapped in a world of bitterness and unforgiveness, unknowingly another puppet in Satan's master plan. We pray for him as a ministry and ask God to soften his heart and to help him see things in a better light.

A ministry "mascot car" used in local parades and events

Blackhawk helicopter landing on property. Three Colonels came to deliver a sermon on leadership for the men in the program.

The men in front of one of our moving trucks, after performing a drama for a parade in Peachtree City

John and Lindsey Barrow at
A Better Way 5 Year Anniversary

Live band at
5 Year Anniversary
celebration

5 Year Anniversary shirts

Living quarters for the men of A Better Way

ABW men at service in a local church

ABW men at Christmas time

ABW Ministry transport vans

Our own street sign

Baptism in the Gulf

Doing discipleship training on the beach

ABW men at the beach surfing

Marrying a new ABW graduate and his wife

ABW men going to church on Sunday morning

Behold, All Things Are Become New
Therefore if any man be in Christ, he is a new creature:
old things are passed away; behold, all things are become new.
2 Corinthians 5:17

The four steps of Baptism

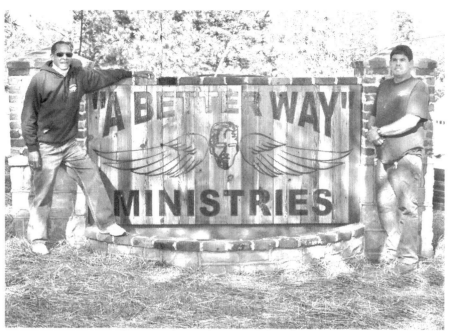

Entrance sign to the ABW ministry location

Charter staff members of A Better Way Ministries
(from left) Jerry Powell, Lisa Neville, John Barrow, Sir Philip Bowden)

CHAPTER 11

APPROACHING THE FINISH LINE

Brother Tony: The Finisher

Well, it wouldn't be right if I didn't share about a great friend and co-laborer. As I said earlier the Lord gave us a great team to start *A Better Way Ministries*. All but one of us are still together. Two years ago we lost Brother Tony who died of a massive heart attack in his sleep. Tony was a trophy in the Lord's showcase of redemption. He was a great example of God's grace and a true disciple of Jesus Christ. In the coming year, Lord willing, we are planning to make a movie about his life, which will be used as a tool to help others find freedom from addiction. Like me, Tony had a very colorful past. He was reared by a Christian mother who prayed for him constantly and an abusive father who was a musician as well as an alcoholic. As a young teen Tony began going to clubs to perform with his dad. He soon became a great musician as well and started a band that eventually toured over half a million miles, cut two gold albums, and was on various TV shows.

Tony, like so many in that line of work, partied hard—drinking, drugging, and womanizing—until one day, at the end of his rope, he cried out to the God his mother knew so well and had so often told him about. Tony quit the band, worked through a program like *A Better Way*, and against all odds went on to Bible College in his 30s, made the Dean's List, and graduated *Magna Cum Laude* ("with high honors"). He then taught music at a local Christian school, played on the worship team at the church, and finished his race helping men just like himself at *A Better Way.*

When Tony passed away I had the honor of doing his funeral. Tony was to be buried in his home state of North Carolina, so we had to plan accordingly. When Tony's family and I were at the funeral home making his final arrangements, the funeral director asked how we planned to transport his body. He offered a few ideas, none of which sounded appealing to the family, so after a few moments of silence, I said very quietly, "I'll take him." They all turned and looked at me with their eyebrows raised and the funeral director said, "I'm not sure if that is legal; let me check." So he got up and left the room and came back a short while later with a quizzical look on his face. "It's legal," he said, "as long as you have the death certificate with you."

So we—me, another young white guy with his baseball hat turned sideways, a black guy from Kenya who spoke with a very thick accent and who filmed the journey as we traveled, Brother Phillip who wore a "city slicker" hat and was from New York—loaded up Brother Tony and headed out for North Carolina. We took him in our 15-passenger ministry van, which by the way had a big fish hook on the side and the words "Fishing for Men," "Casting out into the Deep," and "Discipling men for the Kingdom of God." All these were tied to Luke 5:4, the verse the Lord had spoken to me in the beginning. As we were cruising through one little town after another it hit me that if we got pulled over and a cop read the side of our van, looked at the motley crew of passengers inside, and noticed the huge casket with a dead body in it, certificate or no certificate, we were going to be grounded for a while. Especially if they ran record checks on us. All four of us had records. Think about it for a minute. Four ex-convicts, a huge fish hook, fishing for men, and a dead man in the back.

This will be the opening scene of the movie "The Finisher." The movie got its name from a story I used to tell sometimes when I preached. Tony loved to hear it. It was about the time I was in my attorney-friend's office waiting to close on a piece of property that I was selling. The buyers were

Delivering a eulogy at Brother Tony's funeral

Brother Tony's guitar and flower arrangement

Transporting Brother Tony's casket to North Carolina

The late Brother Tony Ingram preaching a sermon

a married couple who just happened to be missionaries. As we sat there chatting they were telling me about their life as missionaries and about many of their friends who served with them at Operation Mobilization (a missions organization). Every so often the fellow would refer to one of their fellow missionaries as a "finisher" while not saying that when he would talk about some of the others.

So I finally asked him what he meant when he used the word "finisher" to describe a certain missionary. He said, "John, people who were born into missionary families and have been missionaries all their lives are referred to as missionaries, but a *finisher* is a missionary who spends the first portion of his life doing things his own way only to realize somewhere in the middle that his past priorities may not have been in the best order. So he decides to change gears and spend the remainder of his life serving God to the fullest. Hence, the name *finisher*." I will never forget hearing that for the first time because I remember looking at him and saying, "You are looking at a finisher."

Tony dearly loved that story because he wanted so badly to finish well—and he did! Tony's funeral was one of the most moving events I have ever had the privilege of being a part of. We stood a purple Styrofoam heart on a stand down by the casket, and as the funeral began over 50 men—men who were either currently working through the *A Better Way* ministry program or were past graduates—filed down the center aisle of the church and stuck a white rose in that purple heart as they passed by until the entire heart was white. Then several graduates of the ministry shared how much Tony had blessed them by helping them get free of their addiction and become "finishers" for Jesus Christ. There was hardly a dry eye in the room and the service was packed. Tony was surely smiling down on the service from up above and at the way it had ended for him.

It is a story that needs to be told. The movie about his life will do exactly that. It will tell about a man who was lost and then was found, about a prodigal who came to his senses while out in the world searching for fulfillment in all the wrong places. It will inspire multitudes to taste and see that God is good and help many more find "A Better Way."

Please pray that God will continue to get even more mileage out of the life and death of another one of His saints. Brother Tony is now in that great cloud of witnesses right now cheering us on as we "finish" our race.

When You Fall: Get Back Up!

And we need all the cheering and "that a boys" we can get, don't we? Running this type of race can be very wearisome at times. I would have never guessed how much work it takes to run a ministry with over 50 men who are broken, bruised, and in disrepair. It is like being a parent to 50 prodigal sons whom you dearly love. The longer they do well, the more you believe in them. The longer they stay on their feet as they begin to walk out this new life, the more your heart leaps for joy. But quite often (and usually when you least expect it) they will stumble and fall and it will feel as though someone just punched you right in the stomach. It is so painful to watch someone you've grown to love and have pulled for return to the mud once he has been washed clean and restored to his right mind. One thing I have learned over the years is that it takes some time to get all that "stuff" out of you. You don't just get saved and start walking on water overnight.

Brother Tony used to tell a story about when he first got saved. All his ex-band members and old friends would tell him that he had been brainwashed with all that Jesus stuff and Tony would respond with, "Praise God, yes, because I needed my brain washed." Like me, Tony found out very quickly that he was going to need a major cleansing in order to begin to think right. It is in the window of time between the day you get saved and the day you look back and realize that you no longer think like the old lost man that was most susceptible to failure. As I said earlier, Satan is on the lookout for those who have barely began to run and are still trying to get their stride right. He wants so badly to trip you up so that you fall right back into the pit the Lord pulled you out of.

That's what happened with Peter. One day as they were walking along Jesus said, "Peter, Satan has asked to sift you as wheat but I have prayed for you that your faith would not fail, and when you return strengthen your brothers." The word "sift" in Greek (the original language of the New Testament) means "to shake violently, to turn upside down over and over." Does anybody know anything about being violently shaken and being turned upside down in your life? My guess is you do. You see, Jesus was telling Peter that he was going to be tried, just as you and I will, and he certainly was. As a matter of fact, he failed miserably in denying that he even *knew* the Son of God on the night He was betrayed. But notice how Jesus added: "and when you return strengthen your brothers." Jesus was telling Peter and all of His disciples—including you and me—that even though we fall down and make a mistake we must get back up ... and when we do we need to use our fall as an example to strengthen others.

Peter and all of us who are Jesus' disciples must keep running! We must capitalize on the failure and not allow it to be in vain. After we are exposed to our own humanity and weaknesses we must help those around us. What the enemy meant for harm we must now allow God to use for good. Jesus was "cheering" Peter on and inspiring him to "fall forward" in his failure. And he did. Listen to how Peter ended his journey. Peter went on to become the chief spokesman of the early Church as recorded in the book of Acts. He committed the remainder of his life to fishing for men. Tradition has it that Peter was a man with brown eyes dotted with permanent red spots due to his frequent weeping and that he kept a cloth tucked in the top of his cloak at all times to wipe away his tears. Some writers have noted that every morning when he heard the rooster crow Peter was reminded of his precious Lord.

According to early church tradition, Peter was crucified upside down in the city of Rome because he considered himself unworthy of being crucified in the manner in which his Lord was crucified. Concerning the last hours of his life, it is said that when Peter saw his own wife led out to die, he rejoiced because of her summons to join the Lord and called to her by name and very encouragingly and comfortingly said, "O thou, remember the Lord."

Of the Apostle Peter's final days in Rome, Jowett wrote that Peter was cast into a horrible prison called the Mamertine and was confined there for nine months, in absolute darkness, during which time he was manacled to a post and endured monstrous torture. Yet, in spite of his horrific suffering, Peter converted his jailers, Processus, Martinaus, and some 47 others. Peter went to be with the Lord at the hand of the Romans in Nero's Circus in 67 AD.

Christ told Peter that the church would be built upon him (at his confession that Jesus was the Christ, the Son of the Living God) and that the gates of hell would not prevail against it. And that is precisely what happened. No matter how it seems sometimes, *Satan shall not win....* That is the reason we try to go the extra mile with the men in our ministry—because we know that even in the failure there is value. We may not always see the fruit immediately, but we believe that God will have the last word in their lives just as He did in Peter's.

A few years back I was able to take a group of 25 men to New York for the 50th anniversary of Teen Challenge. On the last night of the event as I was walking into the Brooklyn Tabernacle I noticed a man out of the corner of my eye and realized that it was my director, Victor Torrez, who had been over me as a boy some 35 years ago. I couldn't believe it was him. So I walked over to him with all my guys behind me and told him who I was and who I had been back then. I told him how as a rebellious youth I had run away and left his ministry, gotten locked up for selling drugs to an undercover cop, and ended up being extradited back to Georgia. I then told him about my life since then and showed him the guys behind me and thanked him for the major part he had played in my conversion some years later.

At that point Victor started crying. He motioned for his wife and family to join him. He said, "Look, look, this is John and these are his guys. He used to be with us when he was a boy and now look at what God has done." At that very moment I knew that I was in the middle of a divine appointment.

I didn't get it immediately, but when I did it blessed me tremendously. The Lord did two things for Victor right then. He allowed him to see the fruit of his labor and taught Victor and me that just because we don't see the fruit immediately does not mean the tree is dead. God tells us that *our* job is to plant and water and *His* job is to bring the increase. That night was a milestone for both Victor and me. We praised the Lord together, thanked Him for His goodness, and were again reminded that *His word never fails*. It always accomplishes what it was sent to do.

Meeting of former Teen Challenge director at Brooklyn Tabernacle in NYC

In NYC at original Teen Challenge home

David Wilkerson at Brooklyn Tabernacle in NYC

CHAPTER 12

JOB: THE END BETTER THAN THE BEGINNING

TWENTY-FIVE YEARS HAVE passed since I raised my hands in surrender and seven have passed since we started *A Better Way Ministries*. Though I wish I could say that everything has been smooth sailing, well, the truth is, I can't. That would make this book fiction and not a true story. I have found that no matter what kind of Christian you are you will surely have your share of days in the valley. Without valleys, there would be no mountains, and unless you've spent some time in the shadows of the valley, you can't really appreciate the time you spend on the mountaintop. Jesus himself told us that "in this world [we] will have trouble." He also said that we should not worry, however, because He has overcome the world.

The past decade has taught me an awful lot about faith and how, come what may, God's grace is sufficient and His strength is made perfect in weakness. I have had to learn firsthand what Psalm 91 means when it says, "Yea, though I walk through the valley of the shadow of death, I will fear no evil: For thou art with me." The new century began with a frightening diagnosis—one that shook me to the core of my foundation and tested everything I was made of.

Facing a Silent Killer

In May of 2000 a good friend of mine who sold life insurance came to see me and asked if I was interested in buying a life insurance policy. I was, due to the fact that I had none, so I had him sign me up. I then went and got the physical exam required for the policy.

Not long after the exam I received the results of my blood tests. They told me that I had Hepatitis C. At that time I didn't even know what Hepatitis C (Hep C) was. All I knew was that it wasn't good. I sat down at the computer and within seconds found out that I had a silent killer on my hands—a disease that slowly but surely destroys the liver. After reading about the various treatment options for the disease I became quite discouraged. The way I saw it was that you had three doors to choose from and not one of them seemed easy. The first option was to take a drug called Interferon, which made you deathly sick, for an entire year and affected your nervous system. The news went from bad to worse when I learned that the drug had only about a 40% success rate. And to top it off it had to be administered by injection, which was a frightening ordeal for an ex I.V. drug user. It wasn't that I was worried about being tempted to use drugs again, but that I just didn't want any bad memories to surface.

The second choice was to treat the disease with various herbal supplements, dietary changes, and a homeopathic approach—all while hoping for a better medicine to be developed. The odds of the homeopathic treatment option working were about 10%. Not promising at all. The third option was to pray and believe God for a divine healing, which was not something seen every day. I knew that such healing was available to every believer, but it was very rare to see a *true* healing take place.

Because I was very leery of Interferon and its side-effects and believed so strongly in God and His power to heal (despite how rare it was), I figured that I would opt for a combination of the second and third options: I would try the supplements while at the same time seeking divine healing. So for the next few years that's what I did. I tried every natural supplement and every combination of supplements known to man. I flew

2,500 miles across the country to a place called The Healing Rooms in Spokane, Washington, on two occasions. I went to faith-healer Benny Hinn's crusades and even got up on stage with him to blow my Shofar. The elders of the church prayed over me as directed in the book of James.

More hands were laid on me than clap for one of Joel Osteen's corny jokes. I did more fasting than the Jews when they were trying to leave Egypt. One day, three days, five days, seven days, 10 days. Fasting and prayer had become part of my daily life. You name it, I did it. But, for all that, I was not healed of my infirmity. As a matter of fact I grew worse. I finally resorted to the Interferon, which was extremely hard to tolerate given its ravaging effects on the mind and body, making me nervous, edgy, depressed and exhausted. I ended up trying it not once, but four times. It didn't work.

I then did three separate clinical trial studies for new drug treatments. For one study I flew to New York every week for months. For another study I flew to Duke University every week for months. For another I drove from one side of Atlanta to the other for months. I also conducted my own clinical trial with a mixture of various kinds of chemicals that all the Internet "gurus", who mean well but need to stick with what they know, promised would work. It was all to no avail.

When all else had failed I began to pray and ask God to please help someone, somewhere, develop a drug that could kill this deadly virus. And in May 2012 He did. I participated in another study in Marietta, Georgia, and God finally delivered me from that wretched, Satan-spawned disease. It was 12 years to the month when I was finally paroled from Hepatitis C. I can honestly say that prison was easier on me than that virus. When they pronounced me cured (meaning I had cleared the virus and there was no trace of it in my body) I was on cloud nine and felt like a million dollars. My body was not like it was in my 30s, but I felt so much better. I could actually feel the virus leaving my blood as they administered the new drug. The drug is set for FDA approval and is expected to be available by 2014 for everyone. It will just be a few pills, maybe even just one, per day, and it has very few and mild side-effects and only needs to be taken for 8-12 weeks. Hepatitis C will be no more. Praise God!

Many more people have Hepatitis C than we know. It is a blood-borne virus that can be contracted through a blood transfusion, intravenous drug use, tattoos, or any time blood touches blood. It is highly unlikely for someone to get it any other way. There was a big story on the front page of *The Atlanta Journal* as well as on local and national news recently when the Centers for Disease Control (CDC) began urging everyone born between 1945 and 1965 to be tested for the disease. It is known as "The Silent Killer" because you may not know that you have it until it is too late. If you catch it in time and get treatment, your liver has the ability to heal itself and repair any damage the virus has done. It usually takes around 20 years for the disease to progress to stage 4—cirrhosis, a terminal liver disease.

God's Timing is Perfect

A few weeks after being cleared of the virus, I testified of God's good-ness before our congregation at church. I told them how God had finally delivered me and how grateful I was. I also decided that since I had gotten a reprieve from my life sentence I might as well go ahead and get the rest of my body checked out since I probably had many more years of life on earth ahead. Besides I was 50 years old, Hepatitis C had been working me over for 12 years, and I had lived a pretty rough life as a young man. So I decided to start with a colonoscopy. (Such a wonderful experience) The Lord actually told me to get one while I was lying in my bed one morning. I am so glad I listened because they found a polyp that was cancerous. It was a squamous cell cancer in stage two growth. This all happened within 12 weeks of my healing from Hep C and within two weeks of my testifying to my church of God's healing me.

So I had all kinds of tests run— bloodwork, CT scans, MRIs, PET scans, and finally ended up undergoing a month-long chemotherapy and radiation treatment. The doctors had told me I had a 90% chance of being fine, and I truly believed that I would be. Let me tell you why. For the first 24 hours or so after they told me I had cancer I was pretty shaken up. I had just walked out of the woods with Hep C after a 12-year battle, and here I was right back in the weeds again. As before, my first question was "Why, God?... How and why did this happen? Have I done something wrong? Is Satan so bent on killing me? Are all those wrong choices I made as a young man catching up to me now? What is it, God? Am I just snake bitten and doomed for failure? Is it payback time? Lord, please show me and deliver me at the same time."

Well that was the first 24 hours. The second 24 brought an entirely different perspective. After talking to my doctor and other specialists I realized just how blessed I was. They told me that I should be grateful it was caught when it was because otherwise it would have almost certainly killed me. Colon cancer is the second leading cause of death in the U.S., and like Hep C most people don't even know they have it until it is too late. So when I began retracing my steps I started to see the Lord's hand in it all. Had I not cleared the Hep C when I did I would not have gone for that colonoscopy. The only reason I went was that I realized that I probably had more miles to run. Before then I had said I wasn't going to get one because there was "no need to change the tires if the engine was shot." Why worry about a little polyp when I had a ticking time bomb in me anyway?

But because I cleared the Hep C I figured I would get a complete overhaul. If I had not cleared the Hep C when I did I would not have caught the cancer. They told me that we landed on it at about 6-8 months growth. Now what are the odds of that? The Lord not only knew exactly when to clean up one disease but when to reveal the other at its infant stage. If I had cleared the Hep C a year earlier I would have had the colonoscopy when it was too soon to see the polyp. If I had cleared the Hep C a year later the doctors said the cancer would have metastasized and my odds of survival would have dropped to 40%. If I had cleared the Hep C two years later I would have gone on to see Jesus. So looking back, God in His sovereignty knew the day and the hour that He would heal me of my disease. He is perfect in every way! I write this today with a clean bill of health. Both Hep C and cancer free. Praising Him for His goodness!

The Blessing of Prison and Sickness

I have often told my wife that I think everyone should experience prison and sickness at least once in this life. She disagrees, of course, because she has no desire either to be sick or to spend a single night locked up in a penitentiary. My point is that such experiences will serve you well if—*if*—you will allow them to do so. Some of the Apostles Paul's writings would not be here today had he not been in prison with a thorn in his side. In Galatians 4:13 he wrote: "As you know, it was because of an illness that I first preached the gospel to you." Does being confined or sick allow us to receive something that we may not be able to attain otherwise? Does it give us a view from the bottom that often goes unnoticed unless we are forced to our knees? Could it be an opportunity in disguise?

Some may say, "John, are you saying that God would bring sickness or prison on us to help us?" No, I am not saying that, but what I am saying is that God has to allow everything. If it happens He allows it, period. That means that everything is God-sifted and that He is sovereign. And just as Paul wrote so eloquently in Romans 8:28, "All things work together for good for those who love the Lord and are called according to His purpose," which means that good things can and will come from hard times for the believer if we believe and stay focused on the promise.

The truth is that we all get sick in our lives. We may not all get cancer or Hep C or Parkinson's disease, but we all suffer periods of illness. Think back on the last time you were sick with the flu, or a stomach virus, or a bad cold, or had a severe headache. Recall that feeling you had when you began feeling better, when that old flu bug finally left your body or the pain began to ease off. Chances are, you experienced a feeling of gratitude for the relief. There was this feeling of euphoria and you were so glad to be out from under such a heavy load.

All of us are in some kind of prison at one time or another, too—whether it be emotional, mental, or physical. If you've ever experienced a time when you were depressed or discouraged, grief-stricken mourning the death of a loved one, or a romantic break-up, been confined due to an illness, or have actually done time in jail, you have been imprisoned. Think back on that time and recall the feeling you had when you finally got set free? It felt great, didn't it? Those who have experienced such healing and freedom want to sing in the rain and dance in the fields! *Why?* Because we appreciate things more—even normal things like feeling good and being free—and we see the blessings that we once took for granted thereby making us better human beings with softer hearts and a more tender spirit. We are more willing to extend ourselves to others because we have seen the hand of God extended to us. We begin to appreciate what we have and see the value in everything in a much clearer way and are no longer just looking inwardly and thinking about *our*selves, *our* rights, and *our* agenda.

We once had a student in our ministry who got furious at the staff because they did not get the "right" brand of soap for him when they went to the store. He almost quit the program because he didn't get his Irish Spring soap. (The boy wasn't even Irish either. Go figure.) Later that same day we brought in a new student, a homeless man from the streets of Atlanta. He was housed in ole Irish Spring's room as a bunk-mate. That very night Irish Spring asked the homeless man if he needed any soap to bathe with. The homeless man replied, "No, I have plenty." He then emptied his pillow case, which contained all of his worldly belongings, onto the bed and after digging through his small estate he came out with a small bar of motel soap. He held it up and said, "See, I have a whole bar?" Well, I'll let you guess how Mr. Irish Spring felt at that moment. Such situations as this, which prompt us to look around and see just how good we have it in spite of the trouble that Jesus spoke of, change us forever. We then look around and count our blessings and name them one by one. The only way to be of good cheer in the midst of all the trouble is to keep our eyes fixed on Him, focus on what we have rather than what we don't have, and always view our cup as being half full instead of half empty.

One of my favorite quotes is: "I complained because I had no shoes until I met a man who had no feet." Thinking like this will always cause us to stay positive and count our blessings no matter where we are in our life or what we are doing.

Growth Comes Only Through Struggle

I still do not understand all of this and certainly have a lot of questions to ask Him when I get home, but I am convinced that the truth lies in what the Apostle Paul says about all of our trials and tribulations in 2 Corinthians 14: "For our present troubles are small and won't last very long. Yet they produce for us a glory that vastly outweighs them and will last forever." Paul is saying that the things we go through will produce something in us that will last forever—not just as long as we are here on this earth, but *forever*. That means *eternal*. You see God never wastes anything. He would not allow us to go through the trials of life just so they could be used here on earth, but so that we can carry the glory they produce with us into eternity. The seasoning that takes place in us here will be used in and through us forever and ever.

It is like the analogy of the butterfly. One day while playing outside a little boy came across a caterpillar. He picked it up and carried in to show his mom. "Can I keep it, Mom?" he asked, excited. She replied, "Yes, as long as you take good care of it." The little boy got a large jar and put plants in it for the caterpillar to eat and a stick in it for the caterpillar to climb on. Every day he watched the caterpillar and brought it new plants to eat. One day the caterpillar climbed up the stick and began acting weird. Worried, the little boy called his mother who came in and sized up the situation. She understood that the caterpillar was creating a cocoon. The mother explained to her son that the caterpillar was going to go through a metamorphosis and become a butterfly.

The little boy was thrilled to hear about the changes his caterpillar would go through. He watched every day, waiting for the butterfly to emerge. One day it happened, a small hole appeared in the cocoon and the butterfly started to struggle to come out. At first the boy was excited, but he soon grew concerned. The butterfly was struggling so hard to get out! It looked like it wouldn't be able to break free! It looked desperate! It looked like it was making no progress! The boy was so concerned that he decided to help. He ran to get scissors and then snipped the cocoon to make the hole bigger and the butterfly quickly emerged!

As the butterfly came out the boy was surprised. It had a swollen body and small, shriveled wings. He continued to watch the butterfly expecting that, at any moment, the wings would dry out, enlarge, and expand to support the swollen body. He knew that in time the body would shrink and the butterfly's wings would expand.

But neither happened! The butterfly spent the rest of its life crawling around with a swollen body and shriveled wings. It was never able to fly....

As the boy tried to figure out what had gone wrong his mother told him that the butterfly was *supposed* to struggle. In fact, the butterfly's struggle to push its way through the tiny opening of the cocoon pushed the fluid out of its body and into its wings. Without the struggle, the butterfly would never, ever fly. As we go through life, we must keep in mind that struggling is an important part of *any* growth experience. In fact, it is the struggle that causes us to develop *our* ability to fly. And when we fly we know where we are going: Home. And when we get home, we will be flying all the time.

Believe me, I know how hard it can be at times to keep this positive mental attitude and not grow weary and give up and give in to discouragement. But when we stay focused on *home* we can endure the struggles and, like the butterfly, not quit until we shake off that cocoon, knowing that our freedom lies just ahead if we can only break through.

Fighting for the Heart of Our King

The movie *Braveheart* is the fictionalized account of William Wallace who helped inspire his fellow Scotsmen to pursue freedom from the British. Although Wallace sounded the call to arms, it was Robert the Bruce who led Scotland to freedom. Just before Robert the Bruce died in 1329, he asked that his heart be removed from his body after death and taken on a crusade by a worthy knight. His closest friend, James Douglas, honored this last request. So Bruce's heart was removed, embalmed, and placed in a container that hung from his friend's neck. In the early spring of 1330, Douglas was in Spain battling the Moors when he found himself surrounded by the enemy in an ill-fated battle. Once Douglas realized that his own death was imminent, he pulled the heart of his long-dead friend and king from his neck and threw it into the ranks of the enemy. Drawing his sword, he shouted, "Fight for the heart of your king!"

I love that story because it is so like our Christian walk. Jesus counseled us to consider the costs *before* we start to build. We must come to the point where we are "all in" and willing to risk it all based on what we believe. I have found that anything short of that will not get us to where God wants us to be. But, again, this type of sold-out commitment does not come overnight. It is not something that one comes by quickly or easily. It cannot be bought or sold. It can *only* be attained by going through life itself. I tell the guys I minister to all the time that "you get out of it what you put in it," and oh how true that is.

When I was in Jerusalem I went in an old coin shop in the Holy City browsing through the inventory of neat-looking coins. Some bore the image of Caesar, others bore the image of Pontius Pilate, and some were just plain cool looking. All were discovered on archaeological digs and dated back to Jesus' day. So even though I have always been a *lost coin kind of guy*—treasure hunting in the ocean, looking for pieces of eight, gold doubloons, and such—until that day I had never found nor bought one.

As I was scanning the display case in search of the manliest, beefiest-looking coin I could find, my eye fell on this pile of small dainty little coins tucked away in the back, and the Holy Spirit said, "That's your coin, John." So I pretended not to hear Him because I'm not a dainty kind of guy and I never even notice dainty little things in a store. I will never understand how women can spot itsy-bitsy tiny things stuffed way back behind all the huge stuff on a shelf. I notice the big things—the shelves, the roof, the floor, and the walls—but never the *dainty* things. My wife sometimes calls me "oblivious." Any of you guys out there know what I'm talking about?

But this day I did notice, because if you know the Holy Spirit then you know what a "big, loud shout" that still small voice can truly be. He surely can get your attention. So after I quit lusting over all those big manly-looking coins and wiped the drool from my chin, I asked the shop owner about the little girly-looking coins in the box. He told me that they were Widows' Mites. So I asked myself and God, "What does a widow's mite have to do with me?"

Just then I was reminded of the story in the Bible (Mark 12:41-44, Luke 21:1-4) in which Jesus was sitting with His disciples outside the temple treasury watching the people come up to pay their temple taxes and offer their tithes and offerings. Many rich men dressed in fine long robes went up first and put in great sums of money. But then this little old widow walked up and put in two mites, the smallest and least of all the coins—less than a penny in value. Jesus explained what they had witnessed: The little widow, He told them, had out given them all because the others gave out of their abundance whereas the widow gave out of her lack. She put in *all* she had.

Ah, I thought as I recalled that story, *now I get it.*

What I got was this: He was telling me to always give my all and not hold back—to never, ever, give up, to always give my best for Jesus Christ, no matter what it may look like, no matter what comes my way, whether it be trying to love the unlovable, having faith when everything you see screams "failure," moving forward when you were just forced to back up, remaining sick even though you know that Christ is the Great Physician, hopping back up onto your feet with a smile on your face after you were just hit square in the teeth (and sometimes by a fellow Christian or friend).... To preach the word, to testify, to be a light in the middle of a dark place. To be all I can be and to give all I have within me for the sake of the call that has been placed upon me even when I don't have much left to give.

In my life I have experienced loneliness, betrayal, insecurity, prison, Hepatitis C, Cancer, the death of my son, the death of two ex-wives, and the death of many other friends and loved ones. I have had a multitude of bad days and have questioned God on many occasions....

But, I can honestly say that in those times when I was at my worst God was at His best. One plus God is a majority. The most precious times of my life have come in the middle of great pain with Him there at my side. Prison, sickness, failure, being let down—all have been times when the Lord ministered so intimately to me. The truth is, I would not trade anything for the valleys of sorrow because God was with me all the way. Here is a little poem that I ran across one day and sometimes quote to myself:

I walked a mile with Pleasure
She chatted all the way;
But left me none the wiser
For all she had to say.

I walked a mile with Sorrow,
And never a word said she;
But, oh! The things I learned from her,
When Sorrow walked with me.

God not only cured me of Hepatitis C and cancer, but overshadowed all the bad days with good ones. He not only delivered me from every evil thing but has promised that, like Job, the end of my life will be better than the beginning. All of the trials and tribulations I have experienced have produced in me a much more grateful spirit. Gratitude grows out of experiencing the Lord's comforting presence in the midst of the storms and in the darkest valleys. All of the adversity we face in this life (whether it is deserved or not) shapes us into the people God wants us to be—people of sure faith and strong character—and seasons us as believers.

That small coin became mine that day. I wear it around my neck as a constant reminder to give my very best and to have a heart and a faith like that widow, knowing and trusting that the safest place you can put your last two mites of hope is in the palm of His hand, convinced that He will never let you down and that He will surely see you through no matter what it may look like.

Your Opportunity Is Now

Are you in a valley? Do you need help? Are you looking for THE ANSWER? Are you finally ready? Is it a disease—physical, emotional, or psychological pain, a broken heart, betrayal, forgiveness, self forgiveness, or maybe to be set free from prison, physical or emotional? Whatever it is, God will set you free and begin the healing process. He loves you.

Or, if you have never asked God to save you from your sin and give you a new life—a rich full life here on earth and eternal life with God when your time on earth is over—please do so now. It is as simple as confessing your sinfulness, acknowledging that you are sin-broken and need God to fix you, and trusting God to do just that—to save you—based on what Jesus did by taking your sin on Him and dying on the cross for you. You can say something like this in your own words:

> "God, I know that I'm a sinner and that my sin separates me from You, who are holy. I believe that Your Son Jesus died on the cross to save me and set me right with You and that He rose again from death to give me new life! I trust You to forgive my sin and give me new life—now and in the life to come. Fill me with Your Holy Spirit and help me, Father...."

The Bible says that being born again, entering into a saving relationship with God through Jesus Christ His Son, is just that simple. If you prayed that prayer, congratulations. Please drop me a line and let me know so that I can be encouraged as well.

Well, I guess that's it. I could share much more about the journey, but I think I have shared enough for you to get the point. To sum it all up: God is good and His mercies endure forever. He never repays us as our sins deserve and He is always faithful to forgive and to forget. Christianity is "the crutch" that will never let you down.

I pray that reading this book will be a milestone in your life and that it will strengthen you as you travel on. I hope that you will allow it to encourage and compel you, just as Chaplain Ray's books did for me. I pray that what the enemy has meant for harm in your life God will now use for good. I pray that every wasted moment or lost opportunity will be restored. I pray that the Lord will bless you and keep you, that His face will continually shine upon you, and that, no matter where you are and no matter what you are going through, His favor will be yours today.

Be of good cheer, for He is coming soon and He is coming for you.

His Servant,

John Barrow

AFTERWORD

This book was written with a specific goal in mind—to be donated to the penitentiaries and other correctional institutions that house so many hopeless people. The State Chaplain has agreed to help get copies of this book into every prison in Georgia. There are some 200 institutions that house approximately 50,000 men and women. We would like to start with about 10,000 for Georgia and then go out from there. The cost will be somewhere in the range of $50,000 per state, so we need donations to meet our goal. This is a *free* book for people in need as long for as we can afford to give it away. But, of course, it does take funds to print and distribute, so please consider helping us with this endeavor.

All proceeds from this book will go towards helping men and women who are struggling with addiction or who are in prison. If anyone would like to make a tax-deductible donation to our ministry, which is a faith-based 501-c3 not-for-profit organization, you can mail it to us at:

A Better Way Ministries
320 Dividend Drive
Peachtree City, GA 30269

Please earmark it "Better Way Book" so that we will know that you sent because of this request. Thank you.

Also, if you or anyone you know needs help please have them visit our website at: www.abetterwayministries.com or write us at the above address. Our phone number is: 770-631-6202

Barrow family at the beach